# Plough Quarter

T0108398

BREAKING GROUND FOR A RENEWED

Spring 2018, Number 16

Artists: Yvan Lamothe, Roberson Joseph, Barry Moser, Benny Andrews, Zoe Cromwell, Julian Peters, Asuka Hishiki, Mark Smith, Mary Kang, Marc Chagall, John Partipilo, Yuri Kozyrev, Vinicius Barajas, Iain Stewart, Giovanni Bellini

Plough Quarterly

WWW.PLOUGH.COM

Meet the community behind *Plough*.

Plough Quarterly is published by the Bruderhof, an international community of families and singles seeking to follow Jesus together. Members of the Bruderhof are committed to a way of radical discipleship in the spirit of the Sermon on the Mount. Inspired by the first church in Jerusalem (Acts 2 and 4), they renounce private property and share everything in common in a life of nonviolence, justice, and service to neighbors near and far. The community includes people from a wide range of backgrounds. There are twenty-three Bruderhof settlements in both rural and urban locations in the United States, England, Germany, Australia, and Paraguay, with around 2,900 people in all.

To learn more or arrange a visit, see the community's website at *bruderhof.com.*

Plough Quarterly features original stories, ideas, and culture to inspire everyday faith and action. Starting from the conviction that the teachings and example of Jesus can transform and renew our world, we aim to apply them to all aspects of life, seeking common ground with all people of goodwill regardless of creed. The goal of *Plough Quarterly* is to build a living network of readers, contributors, and practitioners so that, in the words of Hebrews, we may "spur one another on toward love and good deeds."

Plough Quarterly includes contributions that we believe are worthy of our readers' consideration, whether or not we fully agree with them. Views expressed by contributors are their own and do not necessarily reflect the editorial position of *Plough* or of the Bruderhof communities.

Editors: Peter Mommsen, Veery Huleatt, Sam Hine. Art director: Emily Alexander. Managing editor: Shana Burleson.
Contributing editors: Maureen Swinger, Susannah Black, Bernard Hibbs, Chungyon Won, Charles Moore.
Founding Editor: Eberhard Arnold (1883–1935).
Plough Quarterly No. 16: America's Prophet
Published by Plough Publishing House, ISBN 978-0-87486-786-2
Copyright © 2018 by Plough Publishing House. All rights reserved.

Scripture quotations (unless otherwise noted) are from the New Revised Standard Version Bible, copyright © 1989 the Division of Christian Education of the National Council of the Churches of Christ in the United States of America. Used by permission. All rights reserved. Images on inside front and back cover courtesy of Iain Stewart, aws / nws, *www.stewartwatercolors.com.*

Editorial Office
PO Box 398
Walden, NY 12586
T: 845.572.3455
info@plough.com

Subscriber Services
PO Box 345
Congers, NY 10920-0345
T: 800.521.8011
subscriptions@plough.com

United Kingdom
Brightling Road
Robertsbridge
TN32 5DR
T: +44(0)1580.883.344

Australia
4188 Gwydir Highway
Elsmore, NSW
2360 Australia
T: +61(0)2.6723.2213

Plough Quarterly (ISSN 2372-2584) is published quarterly by Plough Publishing House, PO Box 398, Walden, NY 12586.
Individual subscription $32 per year in the United States; Canada add $8, other countries add $16.
Periodicals postage paid at Walden, NY 12586 and at additional mailing offices.
POSTMASTER: Send address changes to *Plough Quarterly,* PO Box 345, Congers, NY 10920-0345.

The Prophet We Need Now
Cross, Resurrection, and Beloved Community

PETER MOMMSEN

Dear Reader,

April 4, 2018, marks fifty years since news of Martin Luther King Jr.'s assassination upended American politics and set the nation's cities ablaze with riots. To the two-thirds of Americans who weren't yet born in 1968, including myself, this event seems like the distant past: nearer than the Civil War, maybe, but still just history.

"The past is never dead. It's not even past," wrote William Faulkner in a much-quoted line. The thing is, in regard to this chapter of America's story, Faulkner's dictum is true. King matters too much to be abandoned to dutiful documentaries and corporate wokeness campaigns.

It was King's friend Abraham Joshua Heschel who, in a speech ten days before King's death, publicly proclaimed King to be America's prophet (page 72): "Where in America today do we hear a voice like the voice of the prophets of Israel? Martin Luther King is a sign that God has not forsaken the United States of America. God has sent him to us." Coming from one of the twentieth century's preeminent rabbis and a world-class biblical scholar, this is powerful language.

Or, from another perspective, it's embarrassing – the unseemly lionizing of a flawed man, one with his own set of personal sins and leadership mistakes. Such criticism of King was common already in his lifetime, even among his allies. (Not to mention among his many opponents: in his last years, Americans overwhelmingly disapproved of him, as Gary

Vinicius Barajas, *Easter,* canvas triptych, 2018

Dorrien notes in his article on page 26.) Recent scholarship has highlighted the contributions of the civil rights movement's other leaders and countless grassroots organizers, many of them women activists who never received the respect they were due. This egalitarian impulse, though right and necessary, also has another face. Contemporary culture, with its leveling urge, does not suffer heroes gladly; it eyes any supposedly great person with knee-jerk suspicion.

This issue of *Plough* takes the opposite approach. What if Heschel's words about King are true? What if this name-branded, oft-sanitized, Super-Bowl-ad-commercialized, National-Mall-memorialized preacher from Atlanta . . . is a prophet whose message America has yet to fully reckon with?

"Prophet" is an undemocratic title. We the people can elect legislators and presidents. But God sends us the prophets we need without consulting us. We have no choice but to listen to the fullness of their message, both the comforting and the terrifying. At our own peril we mute those words that disturb the favored pieties of our political, ethnic, or religious tribe.

King's message offers ample opportunities for offense to both left and right. That is because it is so close in spirit to what Jesus taught and how he lived. King's attack on white supremacy, for example, springs not from some secular theory of human rights but from a truth at the core of Jewish and Christian faith: that each human being is created in the image of God. Racism, or any system that judges some humans as inferior, amounts to blasphemy.

Today, King's prophetic clarity about the sacredness of each human being cuts across partisan lines. He shows why white supremacy remains so dangerous, and why there is an absolute right and wrong in how a nation treats refugees and immigrants (pages 18 and 66). He demonstrates that Jesus' nonviolence and love of neighbor can and should be taken literally, even in international affairs (page 56). Taken consistently, his message demands that we protect each human life as inviolable, whether that life belongs to an unborn child, to one of the 2.3 million people behind bars in US prisons and jails, or to a military veteran burdened by traumatic memories (page 11).

King heroically lived out the power of love.

It's this prophetic clarity, and the persistence of the evils he confronted, that keep King's words fresh long after the skirmishes of the 1960s civil rights struggle. Like the oracles of the Hebrew prophets whom King loved to quote, they speak into today's circumstances with stark immediacy.

Of course, King's message is not beyond criticism and correction. The Rauschenbusch-influenced social gospel, which inspired a generation of young idealists in the 1960s, seems creaky a half-century later. King tended to speak of America as if its vocation were that of the church of Jesus Christ instead of that of a mere political body. At times he came close to equating the advance of the kingdom of God with the expansion of federal social programs and civil rights laws, deploying the Bible's language about the age to come as a kind of poetic allegory for national renewal. His vision remains most potent where he hews to the New Testament original, which promises not just social improvement but a new heaven and a new earth. There's an irony in the way social-democratic Christianity, in seeking to apply the gospel as bread-and-butter policy, ends up spiritualizing away the early Christians' most revolutionary claim: that a real flesh-and-blood new creation is coming in which the oppressed will be vindicated, the dead will rise bodily, and all tears will be dried.

None of these objections stopped my grandfather J. Heinrich Arnold, a Bruderhof pastor in the 1960s, from leading the community he was part of to throw its support behind King's movement. "Dr. King is a prophetic voice," he would often say – a line I heard constantly while growing up. To him, it didn't matter that King's voter registration drives meshed uneasily with his own strong Anabaptist convictions on nonparticipation in government (he refused to vote himself). He arranged for Bruderhof members to march with King, and personally responded to King's call to US clergy to join him protesting in Alabama in the summer of 1965. Having experienced the rise of Nazi anti-Semitism in Germany as a young man, he was passionately committed to King's movement for racial justice.

For my grandfather, the decisive thing was that King was heroically living out the power of love – that unlimited, outward-flowing, unconditional love that the New Testament calls agape. This is the love that Jesus taught by commanding that we love even our enemies: "Love your enemies and pray for those who persecute you, so that you may be children of your Father who is in heaven; for he makes his sun rise on the evil and on the good, and sends rain on the just and on the unjust" (Matt. 5:44–45). This agape gripped King – and led to his completely predictable death at age thirty-nine, leaving behind a wife and children ages twelve, ten, seven, and five.

King was living proof that the agape Jesus taught, including his command to "turn the other cheek," is not just an impractical ethical rule that applies only between individuals.

Agape is the strongest force in human life, and it should guide us in all aspects of life, including the social, economic, and political. Far from being an individualistic love, it creates and sustains community. As King wrote in 1957:

> Agape is not a weak, passive love. It is love in action. Agape is love seeking to preserve and create community. It is insistence on community even when one seeks to break it. . . .
>
> The cross is the eternal expression of the length to which God will go in order to restore broken community. The resurrection is a symbol of God's triumph over all the forces that seek to block community. The Holy Spirit is the continuing community creating reality that moves through history. . . .
>
> If I meet hate with hate, I become depersonalized, because creation is so designed that my personality can only be fulfilled in the context of community.

This agape gives rise to the "beloved community" that King so often held out as the goal of his movement. King borrowed the term from the philosopher Josiah Royce. But unlike Royce, for King the beloved community was defined in terms of Jesus' cross and his resurrection, which exclude no one: "When I am lifted up from the earth, I will draw all people to myself" (John 12:32).

In the light of King's lived witness to the heart of the gospel, huge swathes of what has passed for Christianity over the last two millennia are shown to have missed the main point. That's why we still need King as a prophet, not only for America but for the world.

Warm regards,

Peter

Peter Mommsen
Editor

Amish Technology

On John Rhodes's "Anabaptist Technology," Winter 2018: As a fellow Anabaptist from the Beachy Amish tradition, I have always viewed the Bruderhof's cautious approach to technology as one worthy of emulation. I wish

Yumeji Takehisa, *Woman Reading a Book on a Sofa*

to thank John Rhodes for an excellent article. In my own tradition we did pretty well at staving off invasive technology – until the Internet Age, that is. We capitulated when the internet swooped in because we would otherwise have been forced to change, drastically and almost overnight, our approach to commerce. We got caught flatfooted. Perhaps we should have copied our faith cousins at the Bruderhof and worked out a common purse system.

Gideon Yutzy, Dunmore East, Ireland

A Kingdom of Work

On Eberhard Arnold's "The Soul of Work," Winter 2018: At the international office of Word Made Flesh, the ministry where I work, our staff read and discussed "The Soul of Work." Love and work must dance together for community to flourish. In the midst of our tasks and responsibilities, we don't want to forget the reason for our work: love of God and love of neighbor. It's wonderful to see Arnold's vision of integrated work and soul being lived out in Bruderhof communities. At Word Made Flesh, we too seek the humanizing dignity of such holistic rhythms.   *Clint Baldwin, Wilmore, KY*

Silence and the Still, Small Voice

On Stephanie Bennett's "Endangered Habitat," Winter 2018: It is remarkable to consider the vast silence of space before God spoke our world into being, the vast silence of Adam before Eve, and the vast silence of man before his Maker gave him speech. Bennett's piece reminds us of that which we forget almost daily – that silence is actually the ground of our being, and that speech is merely the figure. Organized sound is music. Disorganized sound is noise. When we *noisify* the environment to the degree that we have in technological society, we literally lose the ground upon which the scaffolding of authentic humanness is raised.

Jesus repeatedly removed himself from the crowds to pray, be alone, and be silent. Most citizens of technological society think that alone-ness is synonymous with loneliness. But the Psalmist tells us to "be still and know that I am God": to be alone with God in silent prayer is to never be lonely, but to be comforted in the quiet assurance and embrace of our Maker.

In 1930, T. S. Eliot distilled both the question of our time and its chilling answer: "Where will the word resound? / Where will the word be found? / Not here, there is not enough silence." Perhaps my favorite example of the necessity of silence is 1 Kings 19:11–12: "And, behold, the Lord passed by, and a great and strong wind rent the mountains, and brake in pieces the rocks before the Lord; but the Lord was not in the wind: and after the wind an earthquake; but the Lord was not in the earthquake: and after the earthquake a fire; but the Lord was not in the fire: and after the fire a still, small voice."

Read Schuchardt, Wheaton, IL

Simulating Lent

On Alexi Sargeant's "Simulating Religion," Winter 2018: It is too often forgotten that, even in the midst of their materialism and atheism, the rationalists' basic orientation is to do good and to advance human happiness. For example, giving has become a rationalist obsession; many rationalists tithe or make pledges to donate large proportions of their incomes to charity. Mr. Sargeant is on to something when he writes of the rationalists' efforts to build a sort of church. Many are hostile to religion, but I have experienced, as a student in San Francisco, that rationalists take religious claims far more seriously than your average secular student.

But in the end I am not so optimistic. The rationalists entertain our claims because their philosophy demands that all claims be neutrally entertained . . . except one: reason is a jealous god and he insists that nothing exists above him or beyond his grasp. In the final analysis, the rationalists are simply carrying forward the old lie, first uttered by the serpent: "You will not die. For God knows that when you eat of it your eyes will be opened, and you will be like God, knowing good and evil" (Gen. 3:4–5).

Is it any wonder that many support cryonics? The rationalist Silicon Valley engineer believes in the wrong promise.

Elliot Kaufman, Stanford, CA

Alexi Sargeant responds: I share Mr. Kaufman's worry that there's something satanic in the rationalists' quest for immortality, which is why I look askance at cryonics and mind-uploading. But the *desire* for eternal life is not wicked in and of itself. It's in our God-given nature to long for the defeat of death. Of course it's wrong to seek a manmade eternity, but the presence of that desire in the rationalists should spur Christians to convert them to a true understanding of our destiny in the kingdom of God.

Finally, an intriguing piece of evidence that the rationalist movement is a parallel religion: I recently came across an open thread promoting "Rationalist Lent": forty days of giving up or scaling back one's use of video games, social media, or other practices. When non-Christians display a "holy envy" of Lent, I'm reminded of what a gift the season is. It also reminds me of how much more Christianity has to offer. Our Lent is not a self-improvement regimen but preparation for a real (not virtual) resurrection.

Becoming Immortal

On Michael Plato's "The Immortality Machine," Winter 2018: I would like to clarify Michael Plato's comments about Mormonism. While technology is widely appreciated among Latter-day Saints, transhumanism does not have a strong appeal. I have been a well-read and practicing Mormon for over four decades and had never heard of the Mormon Transhumanist Association until reading Plato's article.

In general, we are critical of novelty. We encourage each other to keep computers in a central location in the home to avoid the temptations of the internet. Many in my congregation in Cedar City have thrown away our television sets altogether. There are exceptions, of course, but to argue that a significant proportion of the Mormon community hopes for a divine future through technology is an egregious mistake.

Samuel Wells, Cedar City, UT

Michael Plato references theosis, the idea that humans will evolve into gods, in a way that may lead readers to think it's unique to Mormon theology. Although interpretations vary among sects and even among their adherents, theosis is an ancient and enduring doctrine among Christians that is broadly, even if sparsely, recognized or acknowledged

Georges de la Tour, Saint Jerome Reading a Letter

among some sects. Mormons call it "exaltation." Eastern Orthodox call it "apotheosis." Catholics call it "divinization." And Christians of any sect that embrace theosis will rightly question the non-Biblical idea that any static conception of human nature is permanently good enough, when it wasn't permanently good enough for Jesus, who exemplifies and invites our transformation into divine nature – to be one with him in Christ.

Almost all Mormon transhumanists would claim to have a goal of immortality, and almost all would claim that we might individually contribute toward achieving that goal. But almost all of us would insist that achievement of that goal also requires a power that transcends us. No one self-attained the laws of physics, the evolution of complex intelligence, or the cultural and technological context that we've inherited. If it's now possible for someone to contribute meaningfully toward a goal of immortality, the possibility itself is pervasive and persistent grace. As Jesus put it, "The Son can do nothing of himself, but what he seeth the Father do"; and yet, "For as the Father hath life in himself; so hath he given to the Son to have life in himself."

Lincoln Cannon, Orem, UT

Michael Plato responds: I did not mean to imply that transhumanism is a majority position amongst the LDS community. I simply meant that, due to certain aspects of Mormon theology, some LDS have found transhumanism very appealing, and have become highly organized and vocal within both the LDS and transhumanist worlds. Yet, as I pointed out in the article, this position is not endorsed by the LDS church.

Regarding Mr. Cannon's comments: while many Mormon apologists have argued that their understanding of theosis has roots in the church fathers and Eastern Orthodox Christianity, the equation does not hold up to scrutiny. Theosis, as it is understood in Mormon doctrine, conflicts with two central tenets of Christianity: monotheism and the doctrine that God created the universe *ex nihilo* [from nothing]. If we ourselves can become gods, then this denies the Bible's repeated assertion that there is only one God. Similarly, the doctrine of creation *ex nihilo* asserts that there is a permanent difference between God and humans, creator and creature.

While some early church fathers such as Irenaeus, Athanasius, Justin Martyr, and Augustine made use of terms such as theosis, deification, and divinization, they meant something quite different. Deification means that we can participate in God's glory, never that we become God in essence. (For a fuller explanation, see the Eastern Orthodox theologian Timothy [Kallistos] Ware's *The Orthodox Church*.) By contrast, Mormonism's doctrine of men becoming gods is unique, and does not accord with orthodox Christianity.

We welcome letters to the editor. Letters and web comments may be edited for length and clarity, and may be published in any medium. Letters should be sent with the writer's name and address to letters@plough.com. ⇘

Faith and Chocolate

In Shell, Ecuador, a small team from the mission organization Reach Beyond is working to develop a hardy cacao plant and to help jungle communities in eastern Ecuador establish it as a cash crop.

Reach Beyond started work in Ecuador in 1931, first with radio broadcasting, then expanding into medical care. But this farming venture is new ground, following a cacao plant distribution drive by the government that did not include instructions on nurturing seedlings. Cacao plants need protection from the region's drenching rains, as they take three to five years to mature. Once established, a families' cacao crop can be grown in fields mixed with shorter-cycle plants such as cassava, beans, and yucca.

In the Reach Beyond program, inhabitants of participating communities own the fields around their homes. They enroll in a continuing education program and will share the profits of all cacao sales, which will be directed to two local factories that process and sell Amazon chocolate.

Wim de Groen, the organization's community development director, describes its work as a parable in action: "We say that 'sharing the gospel is what we do; growing cacao is how we do it.' So as we learn how to care for these crops, we're also reading the Bible and tying it into everything we do. When we graft our cacao plants, we're starting with a root that is very sturdy and can hold on through torrential rains, but the fruit is not good. To that root is grafted a strong and beautiful plant – it grows a bright golden pod and yields dark, high quality cacao. It's a wonderful example of how we need to be grafted to Jesus to bear good fruit."

One of the Reach Beyond greenhouses in Ecuador

Who's Evangelical Anymore?

"Trying to mix Christianity with a political party can be sort of like mixing ice cream with horse manure," Shane Claiborne likes to say. "It might not harm the manure, but it sure messes up the ice cream." At a time when "evangelical" has become a partisan or even ethnic label, many are jumping ship or at least shedding the name. A few who still hope to reclaim the movement's focus on "Jesus and justice" are planning an April revival in Lynchburg, Virginia, home of Jerry Falwell Jr.'s Liberty University. Among those joining Claiborne are Tony Campolo, Jonathan Martin, William J. Barber II, and Lisa Sharon Harper.

Korean Peace Pilgrimage: February–December 2018

Chungyon Won
About one hundred young people have started a pilgrimage to visit cities in South Korea, North Korea (if possible), Manchuria,

Photograph from cafe.daum.net/lordyear

Participants in the 2017 Korean peace pilgrimage

and Siberia to pray for a peaceful future in Korea and beyond. Along the way, participants – most of them members of Bargn Nuri, a Korean intentional Christian community movement – are holding peace- and community-building workshops to meet locals who have suffered in Korea's past wars. They are inviting friends from abroad to join them.

In recent years, Bargn Nuri ("Bright World"), which has a Protestant background, has joined with Catholics and social justice movements in an effort to stand together amid escalating political tension on the Korean Peninsula.

A group of college students founded Bargn Nuri in 1991 in response to social needs stemming from the country's division and rapid industrialization. In 2000, the community settled on the outskirts of Seoul to increase its ministry and educational work. Today, 150 people live within walking distance, supporting each other and raising their children together. They also operate the Christian Youth Academy, offering lectures on history, philosophy, social justice, drama, and culture. In 2010, Bargn Nuri founded a farming village in Hongcheon.

Their commitment to peace is based on the witness of the first Christians. In the words of founder Cheolho Choi, "The early church did not just exist two thousand years ago and then fail. It has

continued throughout church history. The forerunners of faith held on to Christ's peace when wars and violence were rampant. The faith and life of the early church is still continued in community movements today."

The pilgrims met during the Korean New Year holidays to read the New Testament and pray. In March they will travel to Jeju Island, where in 1948 the police and military massacred between fourteen and thirty thousand people, supposedly to suppress a Communist uprising. Although this happened seventy years ago, the truth of this atrocity is only slowly coming to the surface. The pilgrims will walk across the island and hold a memorial service for the victims. In October they plan to visit the North Korean cities of Pyongyang and Kaesong – provided they're allowed to enter the country.

Chungyon Won is the Korean language editor for Plough *and lives at Beech Grove, a Bruderhof in England.*

Poet in This Issue: Naomi Shihab Nye

Born in 1952 in St. Louis, Missouri, to a Palestinian father and an American mother, Nye has always belonged to more than one culture. She spent part of her adolescence in the Middle East before settling in Texas, where she has established herself as a literary voice

of the American Southwest. Nye is the author of numerous books of poems, and her honors include four Pushcart Prizes, a Lavan Award, and a Jane Addams Children's Book Award. ⤳

Photograph courtesy of Naomi Shihab Nye

Photograph by John W. Barry, Poughkeepsie Journal

CHRIS GIBSON

Everyone Should Serve

Former Army colonel and congressman Chris Gibson stopped by Woodcrest Bruderhof, which is in the district he represented in Congress from 2011 to 2017, to talk with Plough *about his new book,* Rally Point: Five Tasks to Unite the Country and Revitalize the American Dream.

Plough: *You've served your country in combat and in Congress. Which accomplishment are you most proud of today?*

Chris Gibson: Of all the responsibilities I have had in my life, being a husband and father is the most important – more important than combat commander, more important than congressman. In fact, I ended my service in Congress after six years because my son needed me at home. If that doesn't go well, then nothing else matters.

I write in my book about revitalizing citizenship; what you are doing here in the Bruderhof community is a great example. The men and women who lead families in this community take their responsibilities as husband and wife, father and mother, very seriously. They look at it holistically: it is not just about preparing children to earn a living but is really about the whole person, starting with faith and spirituality, being a good person morally and ethically, and living up to your potential.

Readers might be surprised to learn that Martin Luther King Jr. was a defining influence on you.

My dad was a manual laborer, a mechanic. When he was working, life was good for us. But when he was out of work or on strike, those were really hard days for our family. We

Gibson visiting Ruth Milliot, the oldest female US Marine veteran, in 2014.

were going through one of these challenging moments when I read in school that Dr. King had gone to Memphis to support striking sanitation workers. His belief that every human life had dignity and that every job had value really uplifted me. He once wrote, "If a man is called to be a street sweeper, he should sweep streets even as a Michelangelo painted, or Beethoven composed music, or Shakespeare wrote poetry. He should sweep streets so well that all the hosts of heaven and earth will pause to say, 'Here lived a great street sweeper who did his job well.'"

As a former soldier you've been active in advocating for war veterans.

As a country, we can always do better for our veterans. Many really need mental health support. Soldiers relish how tough they are physically, so they may be reluctant to seek help for mental health. If you have a broken leg, the idea that you wouldn't go for help is absurd. But if you feel challenged with regard to your mental health, you need help too. So we need a military culture that supports seeking out professional counseling.

My wife works at the Veterans Administration, helping veterans who are dealing with adjustment challenges. I hear from her about their daily travails, which are serious. But I also see examples of neighbors helping – most people are very supportive.

This is one positive development within the last fifty years. The veterans who came home from World War II didn't sleep very well at night either, but they just didn't talk about it. They suffered in silence, and often it came out in other ways: alcohol abuse, substance abuse, and other manifestations.

How can churches help veterans find healing?

Some of these young veterans are only eighteen years old when they find themselves in combat.

They haven't even figured out who they are yet. After we got back to the United States from Iraq, I talked to a nineteen-year-old who was struggling. He said, "Sir, I just don't trust people. Is there something wrong with me?"

I said, "Look, it's no wonder. The things you experienced, we call them unspeakable acts for a reason. There are no words that can adequately describe the things that we witnessed." They were performing their duties in accordance with the law of war, and were serving with honor, but it still impacts them morally. It still impacts their mental health. So just welcome them. When a soldier comes home like this, he or she can feel alienated. Of course, everyone would want to welcome a veteran, but if that effort isn't visually, tangibly made, the veteran may think he isn't welcome. When pastors reach out and say, "Welcome home, I'm glad you are with us today," that is a great first step.

You advocate "peace through strength," or military deterrence. How has seeing the cost of war up close influenced your views?

I'm not a pacifist, I'm a realist. But we have been too quick to use force. I gave everything I had every day as a commander in Iraq, and so did my troops. But I don't think we needed to invade Iraq; that was a mistake. And I don't think we needed to go to war in Vietnam. I believe the Second World War needed to be fought. But whenever a human takes a life, even in honorable service in the military, it is not a natural act. No one who goes to war comes back the same person.

So we need to be much more careful about the decisions we take. We should work for diplomatic solutions at every turn. We should only go to war if we are attacked and as a last resort. Then, if we do go to war, we need to realize that we are going to be supporting veterans for fifty years.

That is not to say that these veterans who are struggling are doomed. Even in the face of significant travail, they have real possibility. There is still hope that they will find healing from moral injury and recover a flourishing life.

With a smaller proportion of Americans bearing the burden of fighting our wars than in the past, do you think an all-volunteer army is a good thing?

I'm torn on this subject, but although there are strong arguments on both sides, I do support the all-volunteer force. For those who are there, it is a very serious business – literally life and death. So it helps the cohesion of the unit to know that they are all volunteers.

Having said that, there were some aspects of the universality of service for the World War II generation that also gave great benefit to the country. We should learn from that. There may be ways we can broaden our view of service. Service doesn't have to be just in uniform. Service also happens when you help your church, your hospital, senior citizens; when you're involved in schools or with firefighters, EMTs, or law enforcement. If we capture that essence of service and look at it broadly, then we can continue to have an all-volunteer military yet as a people harness the positive energy that comes from the shared sense of who we are.

Again, the Bruderhof has been a great example when you've had your young men and women go out into the community to help rebuild after a storm, or when they helped refurbish the Patriots' Home in Kingston so homeless veterans had someplace to live. That is the kind of service we need: real and challenging manual labor but also the spiritual

contribution of being there for veterans who are in a hard place.

In your book you write, "Our most profound problems are not political." What are they then? If Washington can't solve them, where do we start?

We are losing sight of the fact that we are people with souls. We absolutely have material needs. But if you are constantly chasing material things and you feel something is missing, there is something missing: the recognition that we have souls and those souls have needs too. That starts with yourself and your relationship with God. And then we are meant to live with and love other people. We have obligations to our families and friends, and we have obligations to our communities. Right now we are out of balance. At a time when we have never been more connected technologically, we have the highest level of alienation, isolation, and suicide. How can that be? It is because we are racing so fast that we are not even cognizant of these needs that we have and are not fulfilling. ⟫

Elizabeth Washburn, *Solitary Confinement,* oil and encaustic on board

Interview by Sam Hine and Jason Landsel on December 6, 2017.

A Child Named Problem

ODDNY GUMAER

Yasmine with her son in a Bangladeshi refugee camp

Photography courtesy of the author

Myanmar was ruled by a military junta for more than fifty years. Thousands of innocent people lost their lives during the oppressive rule; many more suffered terribly. The Rohingya people, a cultural minority that has historically been oppressed, have been violently attacked and forced to flee from Myanmar into neighboring Bangladesh.

I came into contact with the Rohingya refugees through my organization, Partners Relief & Development, which helps children who are victims of conflict and oppression. Here are two stories that I'd like to share.

Yasmine was nine months pregnant when the army threatened to destroy her home, and her whole village was forced to run. They walked in the heat of the day, constantly looking back to see if the soldiers were getting closer. From afar they could see the smoke of their houses burning. There was no turning back.

She delivered her baby in the jungle that night. The villagers risked their lives to stay with her until the baby was born, but then she insisted that they go: "You need to leave and get to Bangladesh. I will stay here for a bit with the baby and recover." Nobody wanted to leave her, but they knew she was right, and left. Yasmine spent the night alone with her new baby in the jungle, not daring to sleep as she listened for the sound of the enemy approaching. "I was so afraid," she recalls. The next day she got up and kept walking, eventually reaching Bangladesh. She now lives with nine others in a small shack in a crowded refugee camp, where I met her.

She related this story as I held her baby. "I haven't given him a name yet," Yasmine told us, and laughingly added, "I thought I would call him Problem."

I don't know what this little child's life will hold. He lives in an overcrowded camp in a country that doesn't want him, where there is not enough food, water, or shelter to go around. He has no citizenship, no assurance of education, no privacy, and only minimal health care.

But what I do know is this: he is created in the image of God, and I will do my best to make sure the world knows.

Later we visited a family that had just arrived in Bangladesh. They had left everything in Myanmar: their rice fields, vegetable gardens, cows, chickens, cats, and dogs. They had left their houses, blankets, cooking pots, mortars for grinding spices and herbs. They had left clothes, children's drawings, photos, and tools: all those things that give most of us a reason to live. They had nothing left but life itself.

We sat together on an orange tarp, sun striping through the bamboo walls. We didn't speak the same language, so we did a lot of smiling and selfie-taking. The women, who had spent all morning cooking for us, brought out curries, salads, rice, and condiments – a miracle created with so few resources.

Before we started eating, Yusuf entered. He was a head taller than the rest, and his smile filled the room. I was taken aback by his confidence and charisma.

I thought that perhaps he was a UN official. "No," he corrected me, "I fled like everybody else." In fluent English, he explained that he had been working for an NGO that helped children. He had just finished a new house and moved in with his family when the soldiers came. There was no time to plan or pack. They just ran. He told his wife and children to run in one direction and he ran in another, hoping to increase the chance of his family's survival. "I was hiding in the tall grass hoping the soldiers wouldn't see me," he said. "They set all the houses on fire. While I was hiding, I saw them shoot and kill my neighbor's daughter. There was nothing I could do but watch."

Here at the camp, he assists counselors by following up with traumatized children. "They need a way to process all the bad stories in their heads," he explained. I couldn't help wondering what this man could have become, and finally asked him, "What would you do if you could do whatever you want with your life?"

He didn't even have to think about the answer: "I want to help build and strengthen the community here in the camp."

Yusuf is a refugee without even a birth certificate to his name. Still he manages to use what he has and what no soldiers can steal from him – his will to live for something great, something that will last. ⤳

Oddny Gumaer founded Partners Relief & Development (PRAD) with her husband, Steve, and has spent much time in the conflict areas where PRAD works. She is a speaker, author, and mother of three daughters.

Since August 2017, more than 650,000 Rohingya refugees have crossed into Bangladesh from Myanmar.

Were You There?

Children and the Violence of the Crucifixion

MAUREEN SWINGER

Easter Sunday sunrise service at Fox Hill Bruderhof

"I walked the other way. I didn't want my kids to see." My friends were discussing a recent family trip to El Salvador that coincided with Holy Week. They had encountered a procession carrying a statue of Jesus after he was taken down from the cross, and the figure was completely drenched in red paint.

Knowing that my friends were agnostic and perhaps unfamiliar with the Easter story, I felt compelled to point out that Jesus' death *was*

bloody, and that churches across the globe find different ways of commemorating his suffering. They acknowledged this, but . . . "How would you explain such a sight to your children?"

I imagined how the procession must have appeared to my friend – a gory drama depicting an event that she doubts ever happened. Putting my thoughts into coherent order at the moment when they're actually needed has never been my strong suit, but I tried:

Photograph from the Bruderhof Archives

"I don't know how I would explain this to my children. It would depend on the questions they would ask. A bleeding statue would startle any child who has been blessed enough to land in a safe home. But how young is too young to grieve for all innocents who die unjustly, in El Salvador, in Syria, or on a hill outside Jerusalem?

"At some point my children do need to know that innocent bodies bleed and die on our earth, every day. They have never seen violence, real or representative. My husband and I try to talk about suffering in a way that they can take into their hearts without sinking under it. But this sight goes deeper, because we believe that Jesus is real. He did die, and he did live, and that story is the single greatest truth we can pass on to our children."

The conversation ended there, partly because one of those very children hurled himself into our presence, loudly in need of a nap. But that evening, as I tucked the same little boy into bed again, and he was reeling off a roll of all the people he wanted God to remember, I realized that much of what I ought to have said was only then shaping into thought.

I know how the Easter story affected me as a song is a *Via Crucis* by itself, every step causing me to tremble. The version we sing stops at the tomb – it goes no further.

For children who do not yet fully understand the story, these Good Friday traditions are not empty gestures. They remain as symbols in a child's heart until they suddenly become real – the first time we choose consciously to hurt someone, to lie, to betray trust or reject love. Then the patterns live, and we recognize their truth, appearing before we realized our need for it. Tempted to lash out, to dodge the charges or blame someone else, we're instead offered the chance to stop. Be silent. Weep, tremble, and recognize all at once why we need this Jesus: his death, his life.

If we don't know how to grieve, how can the risen Jesus ask us, "Why do you weep?" That sunrise, that empty tomb would mean precisely nothing if there were not first darkness and death.

That sunrise, incidentally, also has a tradition attached. Just before dawn on Easter

The empty tomb would mean nothing if there were not first darkness and death.

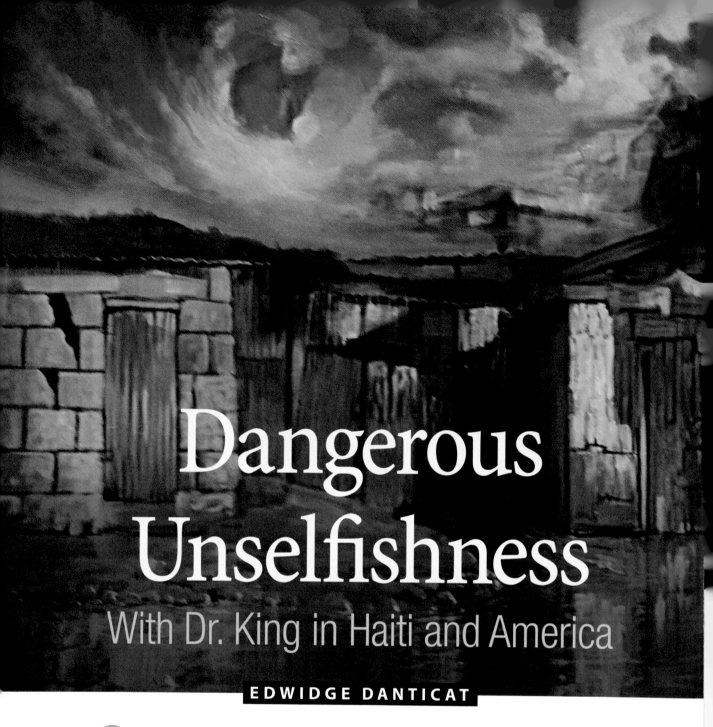

Dangerous Unselfishness

With Dr. King in Haiti and America

EDWIDGE DANTICAT

Some years I celebrate my birthday on Martin Luther King Jr. Day. Though he was born on January 15, and I on January 19, depending on the year's calendar we might end up with kind words being said about both of us on the same day. This year, though, was not one of those times. The Monday of the King holiday fell on his actual birthday and mine followed, just as it should, four days later.

For nearly a decade now, my birthday has been rather complicated. On January 12, 2010, a 7.0 magnitude earthquake struck my native Haiti, nearly destroying most of the capital, Port-au-Prince, and a few other cities

Roberson
Joseph,
Hurricane,
acrylic on
canvas, 2017

nearby. That earthquake killed a reported three hundred thousand people and left one and a half million homeless. Léogâne, the town where my mother, grandmother, and great-grandmother were born, was near the epicenter, and many people I knew there died.

Since the earthquake, January has been an agonizing month, though it begins gloriously with the commemoration of Haitian independence on January 1. On that day, in my family and many others, we drink a delicious squash soup, which was previously considered too

Edwidge Danticat is the author of many books, including, most recently, The Art of Death: Writing the Final Story *(Graywolf, 2017).*

GARY DORRIEN

Redeeming the Soul

# of America

"I am a child of the American white working class. This nation >

African Methodist Episcopal Zion cleric Alexander Walters, anti-lynching crusader Ida Wells-Barnett, and African Methodist Episcopal cleric Reverdy Ransom. They taught that churches had to apply the ethical commands of biblical faith to the political struggle against the tyranny of white supremacism. Their successors included all four of King's chief social gospel mentors: Baptist clerics Benjamin E. Mays, J. Pius Barbour, Mordecai Johnson, and Howard Thurman. King held these mentors in mind when he stepped into the spotlight on December 3, 1955.

King had grown up in a middle-class black Baptist church in Atlanta, where his father was the pastor. He went to Morehouse College at the age of fifteen, moved to Crozer Seminary and Boston University, took over as pastor of Dexter Church in Montgomery while writing his doctoral dissertation, and had a freshly minted PhD when Rosa Parks got arrested on December 1, 1955. King had no activist experience before lightning struck in Montgomery. He had to rely on what he believed and on what his mentors had modeled to him.

Ida B. Wells-Barnett
journalist, suffragist, NAACP founder

Reverdy Ransom
socialist, AME bishop

J. Pius Barbour
Baptist minister

Benjamin Mays
Baptist minister, educator

Howard Thurman
mentor, theologian

Mordecai Johnson
first black president of Howard University

God is the personal ground of the infinite value of human personality. This two-sided credo had a negative corollary that confirmed King's deepest feeling: If the worth of personality is the ultimate value in life, America's racial caste system was evil on distinctly Christian grounds. Evil is precisely that which degrades personality, the sacred dignity of every human life – the very thing that America's racial caste system was designed to destroy. King selected Boston University because its commitment to personal idealism supported his core convictions more powerfully than any other philosophy. Then his ministry in Montgomery put him in position to be swept away by a movement whirlwind.

T WAS THE MOVEMENT that made King, not the other way around. But the movement that carried this young minister to prominence in December 1955 would not have caught fire without him. Montgomery mounted a bus boycott because three organizers had been laying the groundwork for months: Jo-Ann Robinson, president of the Montgomery Women's Political Council; Rosa Parks, secretary of the Montgomery branch of the NAACP; and E. D. Nixon, a former NAACP leader. They were ready to challenge bus segregation when Parks provided the perfect test case by getting arrested. But somebody had to speak for the boycott, and it turned out to be the newcomer who was willing to risk his life. History turned in a moment. King had twenty minutes to plan what he would say that night. He had one guiding thought as he headed to Holt Street Church: *I have to be militant and moderate at the same time.*

"We are here," he told the crowd gathered there, "because first and foremost we are American citizens . . . , because of our love for democracy, because of our deep-seated belief that democracy, transformed from thin paper to thick action, is the greatest form of government on earth."

But American democracy was grievously distorted. Blacks in America were humiliated and oppressed simply for being black. "That's

---

Justice is love correcting that which revolts against love.

---

right!" the crowd shouted. King moved to Parks, lauding her "boundless" integrity and devotion to Jesus. Then he started a justice run: "And you know, my friends, there comes a time when people get tired of being trampled over by the iron feet of oppression."

The crowd erupted in thundering applause, and King kept the run going. People get tired of being "plunged across the abyss of humiliation" and driven into the "bleakness of nagging despair" and "pushed out of the glittering sunlight of life's July." Black Americans were tired of all that, yet they did not advocate violence and never had. "Repeat that!" the crowd called. King stressed that black Americans were Christians who followed the gospel. He tacked back to the right to protest in a democracy. The Klan and the White Citizens Councils terrorized to oppress, while black Americans opposed oppression in the spirit of Jesus. King declared, "There will be no crosses burned at any bus stops in Montgomery." No whites would be extracted from their homes and "taken out on some distant road and lynched for not cooperating." The Montgomery protest sought merely to right a wrong. That got him started on a second justice run. If they were wrong, so were the Supreme Court, the Constitution, Jesus, and God Almighty: "If we are wrong, justice is a lie. Love has no meaning. And we are determined here in Montgomery to work and fight until justice runs down like water and righteousness like a mighty stream."

King moved from quoting the prophet Amos to a call for solidarity: "We must stick together." The movement needed unity and courage, the one reinforcing the other. He risked a trade union analogy, observing that when working people got "trampled over by capitalistic power," there was nothing wrong with pulling together to demand their rights. "We, the disinherited of this land, we who have been oppressed so long, are tired of going through the long night of captivity. And now we are reaching out for the daybreak of freedom and justice and equality."

Rosa Parks
activist, organizer

Jo Ann Robinson
organizer, educator

E. D. Nixon
union organizer, activist

The crowd erupted again at the stunning image of daybreak. King implored the crowd to "keep God in the forefront." But love, he said, is only one side of the Christian faith; the other side is justice. Christians live in the spirit of love divine *and* employ the tools of divine justice. They use the tools of persuasion *and* the tools of coercion. If they pulled together, history would be written in Montgomery.

King ran out of metaphors, halting his run, but the Holt Street Address perfectly distilled what became his message: "Justice," he said, "is love correcting that which revolts against love." Soon this message was his trademark, helping him to personally link the fledgling, theatrical, church-based movement for racial justice in the South to the established, institutional, mostly secular movement in the North.

BLACK PACIFIST ACTIVIST Bayard Rustin rushed to Montgomery from New York, befriended King, and introduced him to his fellow Old Left activists Stanley Levison and Ella Baker. After the boycott succeeded, all four were determined to build a new organization that would kindle many Montgomerys. The NAACP still had a role to play, but it was consumed with marching through the courts. The Congress on Racial Equality (CORE) protested bravely and doggedly, but failed to spark a movement. It was top-heavy with white middle-class intellectuals who gave an impression of patronizing earnestness. Another version of CORE was not what the movement needed.

The new organization would be exclusively black, but its goal was to redeem the entire nation. In December 1956 King told a celebratory gathering at Holt Street Church that the goal was to "awaken a sense of shame within the oppressor and challenge his false sense of superiority," not to defeat white oppressors: "The end is reconciliation; the end is redemption; the end is the creation of a beloved community." The following month King, Birmingham minister Fred Shuttlesworth, and Tallahassee minister C. K. Steele called for a conference to establish a new organization. By August 1957 it had a name, the Southern Christian Leadership Conference (SCLC), and a motto: "To Redeem the Soul of America."

King rightly figured that the movement needed a church-based organization dedicated to spreading protest wildfire. He stocked SCLC with powerhouse preachers who deferred to him; meanwhile he relied on Rustin and Levison for ghostwriting, networking, and counsel and hired Baker to run the office. Rustin, Levison, and Baker were veterans of the Old Left who fondly remembered how the Congress of Industrial Organizations (CIO) used strikes, boycotts, and marches to make gains for economic justice. They were also chastened by this history, because the Old Left strategy of fusing anti-racism with trade unions and socialism had failed in the 1930s and '40s. Racism cut deeper than class solidarity.

Thus the three movement veterans were strategic in basing SCLC on the black church, notwithstanding that Rustin was a socialist Quaker, Levison was a Jewish former Communist, and Baker's experience of the black church made her averse to authoritarian preachers. SCLC embraced nonviolence and touted its political nonpartisanship, although Baker accepted nonviolence merely as a tactic, not as the faith it was for Rustin and King. The SCLC ministers and board members did not like King's reliance on Rustin and Levison, but King was emphatic about needing them.

King took in stride that Rustin, Levison, and Baker had Old Left backgrounds. It was one of God's mysteries why so many Communists and so few white liberals had cared about black Americans. King had become a democratic socialist in seminary, embracing the conviction of Johnson, Barbour, social gospel icon Walter Rauschenbusch, and Boston University ethicist Walter

Bayard Rustin
activist, strategist

Stanley Levison
lawyer, advisor, speechwriter

Ella Baker
advisor, organizer

Fred Shuttlesworth
Baptist minister, organizer

C. K. Steele
Baptist minister, organizer

Muelder that political democracy cannot survive without economic democracy. Then he joined a racial justice movement in which he took for granted that former Communists had major roles to play. Rustin and Levison believed that black Americans would never be free as long as large numbers of whites were oppressed by poverty. Capitalism, they said, played different roles in the struggles for racial justice in the North and South. In the North, blacks suffered primarily from the predatory logic of capitalism. In the South, blacks suffered primarily from the tyranny of racial caste, and capitalism was an ally in the struggle against racial tyranny because the capitalist class experienced the demands of racial caste as a needless waste. In the North, fighting for economic justice was intrinsic to the struggle for racial justice; in the South, economic justice was secondary for the time being. King agreed with Rustin and Levison that the Northern and Southern struggles had to be waged differently *and* that the struggle for economic justice for *all* Americans was indispensable in the long run.

FOR A WHILE, SCLC floundered, even as King became famous. King shuddered to imagine the violence that Gandhian protests might unleash; thus he talked about Gandhian disruption without causing any. It took the student sit-in explosion of 1960 and the founding of the Student Nonviolent Coordinating Committee (SNCC) to push King into committing Gandhian disruption. King accepted that he needed to raise hell in the most hostile cities he could find. SCLC became a fire-alarm outfit relying on street theater and heroic agitation. It was long on charismatic ministers who disdained grassroots organizing and did not treat their female allies with the respect they deserved. King was no exception on either count; thus Baker left SCLC to advise SNCC. But both organizations stoked the fires of protest in ways that King's leadership inspired.

From 1960 until his death, King got more radical and angry in every succeeding year. The great demonstration in Birmingham was excruciatingly slow to catch fire, saved by marching children, and nearly ended disastrously, but it caused President Kennedy to propose the Civil Rights Act. In 1964, interviewer Alex Haley asked King what his biggest mistake had been, and King said it was overestimating the spiritual integrity of white ministers. The essence of Pauline

We domesticated King in order to win for him the iconic status he deserves.

Christianity, he observed, is to rejoice at being deemed worthy to suffer for the divine good: "The projection of a social gospel, in my opinion, is the true witness of a Christian life." The white ministers who opposed or sat out the civil rights movement failed the Pauline test. Haley asked if black churches did better at projecting a social gospel; King hedged on "no," adding that black churches dealt with daily threats to their existence that whites couldn't imagine, so there was no basis for comparison.

Haley noted that many derided King as a sell-out; King said he took for granted that criticism came with the job. Haley asked how one could be militant and nonviolent at the same time; King said it was a necessity, like being simultaneously realistic and idealistic. Nonviolence is a sword that heals. Haley

Walter Rauschenbusch
theologian, Baptist minister

Walter Muelder
ethicist, ecumenist, theologian

observed that many whites believed the civil rights movement had gone far enough and should cease. King's response was blistering: "Why do white people seem to find it so difficult to understand that the Negro is sick and tired of having reluctantly parceled out to him those rights and privileges which all others receive upon birth or entry in America? I never cease to wonder at the amazing presumption of much of white society, assuming that they have the right to bargain with the Negro for his freedom. This continued arrogant ladling out of pieces of the rights of citizenship has begun to generate a *fury* in the Negro."

The fury in King showed through to anyone willing to see it. He said that white Americans were abysmally ignorant about the true state of American society, and three variations of this ignorance were politically significant. One group was stridently bigoted and reactionary; a second group, public officials, did not fathom the harm they caused, because it never occurred to them to actually listen to black people; a third group was the hardest to take, "enlightened" types who admonished in patronizing fashion about proceeding gradually.

Selma nearly ended disastrously, but the march to Montgomery led to the Voting Rights Act. Then King took the struggle North, where very few of his lieutenants wanted to go. King said that racism in the North was structural and threefold in every city. Segregated housing led to segregated schools, and segregated housing and schools handicapped black Americans in the job market. So he pushed into Chicago, where SCLC was battered viciously. This time the battering was not redeemed by any national legislative breakthrough, just before Watts and Detroit exploded in rioting.

Until 1966, King refused to say that white Americans never intended to integrate their schools and neighborhoods. Then he got pelted with rocks in Chicago and said it scathingly, cautioning the SCLC: "The white man literally sought to annihilate the Indian. If you look through the history of the world this very seldom happened." This, he said, was what black

The fury in King showed through to anyone willing to see it.

Americans were up against. Until 1967, King refused to describe white America's reaction to the civil rights movement as a backlash, because that kind of language suggested that he was to blame, racism was increasing, and the movement had backfired. Then King wrote his last book, *Where Do We Go from Here,* and he stopped imploring against calling it a backlash. The backlash was terribly real, he said, but what mattered was the cause: America's age-old racial hostility. The civil rights movement merely brought this hostility to the surface. Coping with that reality was, and is, a spiritual discipline.

Hope gives power to the way of nonviolence; thus King accepted the burden of being a bearer of hope, even as he stressed that white supremacy vengefully prevailed. He warned that despair never sustained any revolution. Liberation and integration go together, and must do so, because power must be shared in a just society. The sharing of power is the very definition of a just society. King wearied of being asked if he still believed in nonviolence. He reached for a way of saying it that settled the question. Most black Americans, he believed, agreed with him about nonviolence, but even if they did not, he believed in it. Some leaders merely reflect whatever the consensus happens to be. King took no interest in that. For him it was convictional leadership or bust, and his conviction was a burning fire in him: "Occasionally in life one develops a conviction so precious and meaningful that he will stand on it till the end. That is what I have found in nonviolence."

VERY NEAR THE END OF HIS LIFE, in his last Christmas sermon, King made his usual vow to endure suffering, respond to violence with soul force, and love the oppressors. But now he said it by counterposing the dream of a just society with the nightmares of recent years: the four girls murdered in a church in Birmingham, the miserable poverty of urban neighborhoods, American cities on fire, the war in Vietnam. At the end, King was unfathomably exhausted, living on the edge of despair. But he did not give in to it. "Yes, I am personally the victim of deferred dreams, of blasted hopes, but in spite of that I close today by saying I still have a dream, because, you know, you can't give up in life."

In his last years King fixed on three reforms, one movement ambition, and one colossal imperative. The reforms were to terminate racial discrimination in housing, establish a minimum guaranteed income, and end America's militarism. The movement ambition was to build a multiracial "Poor People's Movement" for social justice. One of King's favorite stories on this subject took place during his jail experience in Birmingham. He told it in his last sermon at Ebenezer Church, two months before he died:

> The white wardens and all enjoyed coming around the cell . . . showing us where we were so wrong demonstrating. And they were showing us where segregation was so right. . . . And then we got down one day to the point . . . to talk about where they lived and how much they were earning. And when those brothers

told me what they were earning, I said, "Now, you know what? You ought to be marching with us. You're just as poor as Negroes." And I said, "You are put in the position of supporting your oppressor, because through prejudice and blindness you fail to see that the same forces that oppress Negroes in American society oppress poor white people."

King took for granted that the movement for social justice had to give high priority to influencing the federal government. Every reform that he sought focused on the federal government. He never believed that passing the Civil Rights Act and the Voting Rights Act exhausted the struggle for government reforms. Though King lost President Johnson's support after he condemned the Vietnam War in April 1967, he did not make a fetish of the outsider status to which he was driven. The civil rights bills had to be defended and enforced, he wanted the ear of the next president, and it mattered greatly what kind of role the federal government played in social

Martin Luther King Jr. sits in his cell at the Birmingham City Jail, Alabama, October 1967.

issues, human rights, and war. Believing that a minimum guaranteed income was the appropriate successor to the civil rights bills, King threw his heart and soul into that cause, whether or not a civil rights bill focused on housing could be revived.

Photograph by Dick DeMarsico from Wikimedia Commons (public domain)

The Handwriting on the Wall

We have come here
    because we share a common concern
        for the moral health of our nation.
We have come because our eyes
    have seen through the superficial
        glory and glitter of our society
    and observed the coming of judgment.
Like the prophet of old, we have read the handwriting on the wall.
We have seen our nation weighed in the balance of history
    and found wanting. . . .

Cowardice asks the question, is it safe;
expediency asks the question, is it politic;
vanity asks the question, is it popular;
but conscience asks the question, is it right?

And on some positions, it is necessary
    for the moral individual to take a stand
that is neither safe, nor politic, nor popular;
    but he must do it because it is right.

Source: Martin Luther King Jr., "The Three Evils of Society," speech at the National Conference on New Politics in Chicago, August 31, 1967.

Giovanni Bellini, *Pietà Martinengo*, 1505

Liberation at the Cross

OSCAR ROMERO

Thirty-eight years ago, El Salvador's Archbishop Oscar Romero fell to an assassin's bullet while celebrating Mass. In life, his outspoken call for justice for the poor earned him the accusation of political meddling and even of supporting Communism. Now the Vatican is close to declaring him a saint. It's not hard to see why: though he never shied from confronting oppression, his message was grounded in a profound love for the nonviolent Christ. Here are his words, taken from a new Plough *collection of his writings and sermons titled* The Scandal of Redemption *(see next page).*

THERE CAN BE NO FREEDOM as long as there is sin in the heart. What's the use of changing structures? What's the use of violence and armed force if the motivation is hatred and the purpose is to buttress those in power or else to overthrow them and then create new tyrannies? What we seek in Christ is true freedom, the freedom that transforms the heart, the freedom the risen Christ announces to us today, "Seek what is above" (Col. 3:1). Don't view earthly freedom and the oppression of this unjust system in El Salvador just by looking down from the rooftops. Look on high! That doesn't mean accepting the situation, because Christians also know how to struggle. Indeed, they know that their struggle is more forceful and valiant when it is inspired by this Christ who knew how to do more than turn the other cheek and let himself be nailed to a cross. Even submitting to crucifixion, he has redeemed the world and sung the definitive hymn of victory, the victory that cannot be used for other ends but benefits those who, like Christ, are seeking the true liberation of human beings. This liberation is incomprehensible without the risen Christ, and it's what I want for you, dear sisters and brothers, especially those of you who have such great social awareness and refuse to tolerate the injustices in our country. . . . Lift your hearts on high, and consider the things that are above!

> Here is the proof that love alone solves everything.

DEAR YOUNG PEOPLE given to violence and vice, you who have already lost your faith in love and think that love can solve nothing, here is the proof that love alone solves everything. If Christ had wanted to impose his redemption through armed force or through fire and violence, he would have achieved nothing. That would have been useless; there would be only more hatred and wickedness. But going straight to the heart of redemption, Christ tells us on this night, "This is my commandment: as I have loved you, so you also should love one another." And he says more: "So that you may see that these are not simply words, stay with me tonight when I will sweat blood as I observe the evil of humankind and the pain of my own sufferings! And tomorrow you will see me carrying the cross like a silent lamb and dying on Calvary. Be assured that I bear no resentment toward anybody. From the depth of my soul I will cry out, 'Father, forgive them, they know not what they do.'" Let us reflect, sisters and brothers, on this personified gesture of love. And when we are tempted to act with vengeance, resentment, cruelty, or selfishness, let us not consider the sad example of people who hate one another. Rather let us raise our eyes toward the love that becomes lamb, that becomes food, that becomes Passover, that becomes covenant.

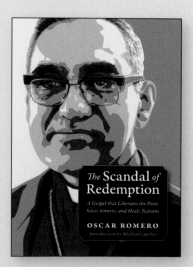

Hard Work, Not Complacency

It may well be that we will have to repent
    in this generation
not merely for the vitriolic words
    and the violent actions of the bad people,
but for the appalling silence
    and indifference of the good people
        who sit around and say wait on time. . . .

Social progress never rolls in
    on the wheels of inevitability.
It comes through the tireless efforts and the persistent work
    of dedicated individuals.
And without this hard work
    time itself becomes an ally
        of the primitive forces of social stagnation.

And so we must help time. We must realize
    that the time is always right
        to do right. ➤

Source: Martin Luther King Jr., "The Other America," speech at Stanford University, April 14, 1967.

POWERSan

King and the Holy Spirit

AND WHY TODAY'S ACTIVISTS NEED THE POWER OF PENTECOST

EUGENE F. RIVERS III

The night before his death, Martin Luther King Jr. preached his last sermon in Mason Temple. A monumental brick-and-stone edifice in downtown Memphis, Mason Temple is the mother church of the second-largest black denomination in the United States, known as the Church of God in Christ. Near where King was standing was the marble tomb of the church's founder, Bishop Charles Harrison Mason, who had been born a slave and had gone on to become black America's foremost Pentecostal leader.

Pentecostalism, now the fastest-growing branch of Christianity, emphasizes the power of the Holy Spirit to transform every aspect of the believer's life. The movement originates in the multiracial Azusa Street Revival in Los Angeles in 1906. Just months after the revival began, Mason traveled to California to see what was happening with his own eyes; it proved to be the turning point of his life. As Mason would later recount, "The Spirit came upon the saints and upon me. . . . Then I gave up for the Lord to have his way within me. So there came a wave of glory into me and all of my being was filled with the glory of the Lord."

Mason, having now been "baptized with the Holy Spirit," as Pentecostals describe such a conversion experience, became a fearless evangelist for the new movement. By the time of his death seven years before King's sermon, the Church of God in Christ counted four hundred thousand members in four thousand churches in the United States and around the world.

Your Sons and Daughters Will Prophesy

This sanctuary, then, was the place in which King rose to deliver his farewell "Mountain Top" address: at an epicenter of global Pentecostalism. In retrospect, this seems powerfully symbolic. For Pentecostals, a central scripture is the promise of the prophet Joel, which the apostle Peter quoted at the first Christian Pentecost in Jerusalem: "I will pour out my Spirit on all people and your sons and daughters will prophesy, and your old men will dream dreams and your young men will see visions" (Joel 2:28). Heard in this context, King's last sermon can be understood as a fulfillment of this ancient promise. He, too, was one on whom the Holy Spirit had been poured out, one empowered with the gift of prophecy.

As we mark a half century since King's death, few tributes acknowledge that the spiritual and political movement he led was a movement of the Holy Spirit. Yet secular accounts of his life and message are inadequate to explain what happened to and through him. Nor do they recognize that the forces he opposed – white supremacy, economic oppression, and militarism – are spiritual realities in

Rev. Eugene F. Rivers III and his wife, Dr. Jacqueline Rivers, are executive directors of the Seymour Institute on Black Church and Policy Studies at Harvard University.

their own right, demonic powers that must be combatted with spiritual weapons. As the New Testament puts it, "Our struggle is not against flesh and blood, but against the rulers, against the authorities, against the powers of this dark world and against the spiritual forces of evil in the heavenly realms" (Eph. 6:12).

This is not just a matter of historical interest. Whether or not the Holy Spirit inspires our political and cultural activism is of urgent importance today. The virulence of white supremacist discourse is at a new low, while white supremacist action is at a new high, with innocent people being attacked in Charlottesville, Virginia, and at Mother Emanuel Church in Charleston, South Carolina. This reality demands that the church reclaim the power of the Spirit to discern the most effective response. We must name, unmask, and engage the invisible powers that threaten human existence.

King the Christian

Throughout the 1960s, King waged a political struggle against the macrostructural forces arrayed against black people. His genius was to recognize the power of the black church for organizing resistance to white supremacy, a dynamic that none of the secular intelligentsia had foreseen. None of the social scientists, black or white – W. E. B. Du Bois, E. Franklin Frazier, Gunnar Myrdal, Arthur Schlesinger Jr. – had predicted this. King insisted that the word Christian be part of the title of what was

originally the Southern Leadership Conference, because he knew that blacks in the South would be strengthened by Christian solidarity, and that for them the church would be the most powerful organizing base. The Southern Christian Leadership Conference went on to become one of the leading institutions in the civil rights movement.

Just as insightful was King's commitment to the Christian ethic of love, based in the teachings of Jesus. In his Sermon on the Mount, Jesus taught nonviolence, love of enemy, and unconditional forgiveness. For King, Jesus' way of love had a deep kinship with the strategy of nonviolent resistance that he learned from Mahatma Gandhi.

There is no doubt that King sincerely believed in the principles of nonviolent action. But the strategic brilliance of using Gandhi's methods is also unquestionable. In the American South, with its terrorist, totalitarian Jim Crow regime, nonviolence was the perfect weapon.

The gains that the civil rights movement achieved as a result were unprecedented – and God-given. Yet by the end of the 1960s, King's reliance on Gandhian ethics alone was proving insufficient. A Protestant liberal by training, he was only dimly aware of the invisible principalities and powers that lay behind the violence of white supremacy. In the end, this restricted theological vision limited the longevity of the movement and its ability to adapt to radically different political circumstances, such as urban life outside of the South.

The Influence of Liberal Theology

Martin Luther King Jr.'s liberalism, in fact, might be seen as an accidental byproduct of the supremacist totalitarianism of the American South. Raised in his father's church in Atlanta, Ebenezer Baptist Church, he was taught to believe in the authority of the Bible. But his understanding of the New Testament's teaching about the Holy Spirit, with all its potential political implications, remained underdeveloped. He was educated at Morehouse College, the favored institution for the training of elite black men, where he was mentored by the legendary but theologically liberal Benjamin E. Mays.

He then went on to Crozer Theological Seminary in Upland, Pennsylvania, where he absorbed the theological liberalism of 1950s Northern Protestantism. Here he was taught a low view of biblical authority – and a suspicion of the miraculous and supernatural. The historian Taylor Branch, in the first volume of his Pulitzer Prize–winning trilogy, *Parting the Waters,* captures the theological world of the young King as a Crozer seminarian. The standing joke among Crozer students who survived the first term was that "the biblical image of Moses was destroyed in the first term and Jesus was finished off in the second." This milieu distanced King from a purely biblical vision of the Holy Spirit.

There is, however, more to this story of King's theological evolution. In the 1950s South, theologically conservative seminaries, regardless of denomination, were largely segregated. Unlike Northern seminaries, they claimed to hold a high view of the Bible – and used it to justify Jim Crow by interpreting Noah's curse on his son Ham's descendants as referring to blacks. Thus, they espoused young earth creationism while also, with rare exceptions, tolerating if not endorsing the terrorist program of the Ku Klux Klan.

Herein lies an amazing irony, that the racism of white Southern seminaries drove the most talented future black leaders to integrated Northern seminaries, which were at least less explicitly racist. In this way, conservative Christians' sin of white supremacy planted the seeds of resistance in the hearts of a rising generation of black church leaders. Not surprisingly, however, these precocious black students emerged with a decidedly liberal theological and social orientation. Thus, for the first half of the twentieth century, the intellectual leadership of the black church would be educated in an environment that inhibited them from fully tapping into the Pentecostal movement's radically biblical vision of the power of the Holy Spirit.

The Movement after King

The failure of King and his church-based movement to fully recognize the spiritual character of the unraveling of a coherent political left during the sixties had significant cultural consequences. During the next decade, various forms of an ingenious and complex art form, hip-hop and rap, emerged. It spoke as much to the pain of devastated inner cities as to the creativity of those who had been abandoned there.

Christian philosopher Cornel West provides a brilliant and important analysis of this environment. In his book *Race Matters* he asserts, correctly, that "the proper starting point for the crucial debate about the prospects for black America is an examination of the nihilism that increasingly pervades black communities." He then proposes a definition: "Nihilism is to be understood here not as a philosophic doctrine that there are no rational grounds for legitimate standards or authority; it is far more the lived experience of coping with a life of horrifying meaninglessness, hopelessness, and most important, loveless-ness. The frightening result is a numbing detachment from others and a self-destructive disposition toward the world." His analysis finds its most creative empirical confirmation in the words of Grandmaster Flash's classic, "The Message":

> You'll grow in the ghetto livin' second-rate
> And your eyes will sing a song called deep hate
> The places you play and where you stay
> Looks like one great big alleyway
> You'll admire all the number-book takers
> Thugs, pimps and pushers and the big money-makers . . .
> And you'll wanna grow up to be just like them, huh . . .
> Turned stick-up kid, but look what you done did
> Got sent up for a eight-year bid . . .
> 'Til one day, you was found hung dead in the cell
> It was plain to see that your life was lost

> You was cold and your body swung back and forth
> But now your eyes sing the sad, sad song
> Of how you lived so fast and died so young.

Such an attitude of nihilism reflects the triumph of the demonic in the surrounding culture. What, then, is to be done about it? West, drawing on the teachings of Jesus, proposes an answer: "If one begins with the threat of concrete nihilism, then one must talk about some kind of politics of conversion. . . . Nihilism is not overcome by arguments or analyses. It must be tamed by love and care."

West understands that a "love ethic must be at the center of the politics of conversion." One needs the supernatural power of God to resist the power of the evil one and to accomplish the transformation required to live a life of love. At this moment in history, the church must once again engage in the spiritual warfare that will transform society and renew culture.

To Demolish Strongholds

The spiritual reality of the civil rights struggle was grasped early on by the theologian William Stringfellow. At the first National Conference on Religion and Race in 1963 – where King, Sargent Shriver, and Abraham Joshua Heschel also spoke – Stringfellow argued that white supremacy had to be understood as a demonic principality. This conference was the first time mainline denominations seriously engaged the freedom struggle, and Stringfellow's remarks were controversial, especially his excoriation of

"The weapons we fight with
On the contrary, they
to die

the meeting as "too little, too late, and too lily white." But just as provocative was the following claim:

> The monstrous American heresy is in thinking that the whole drama of history takes place between God and humanity. But the truth, biblically and theologically and empirically, is quite otherwise: The drama of this history takes place amongst God and humanity and the principalities and powers, the great institutions and ideologies active in the world. It is the corruption and shallowness of humanism which beguiles Jew or Christian into believing that human beings are masters of institution or ideology. Or to put it differently, racism is not an evil in human hearts or minds; racism is a principality, a demonic power, a representative image, an embodiment of death over which human beings have little or no control, but which works its awful influence in their lives.

In asserting this, Stringfellow advanced a much more radical understanding of the nature of racial injustice in the United States and implicitly proposed a more Pentecostal reading of these historical events.

What Stringfellow missed, however, is something that the former slave Bishop Mason would have pointed out: that human powerlessness in the face of demonic racism is transformed into potency by the power of the Holy Spirit. This is not the power of the Holy Spirit as an abstract concept. Rather, it is the power of the Holy Spirit that Luke describes in the Book of Acts with the occurrence of miraculous signs and wonders, and that Paul refers to in 1 Corinthians 2: "My message and my preaching were not with wise and persuasive words, but with a demonstration of the Spirit's power, so that your faith might not rest on human wisdom, but on God's power."

Although I am sure that in many of the churches in Montgomery and Birmingham and throughout the South, particularly in the small churches of the poor, there were saints engaged in Spirit-filled intercessory prayer, more of that power would be needed as King moved to larger cities where he encountered more powerful territorial spirits. In opposing white supremacy in small cities, the prayers of scattered believers invoking the Holy Spirit proved adequate. But in a larger metropolis much greater power would have been needed. To say this is not to dismiss the impact of institutional and structural factors on the movement in large cities. From a spiritual perspective, these structural forces are an integral part of the operation of the demonic principalities.

To the extent that a biblical conception of supernatural forces informed King's analysis of the challenges he faced and his strategic decisions regarding the direction of the movement, this aided his success. And whenever the movement failed to reckon with the entrenched principalities it was up against, this contributed to its failures.

re not the weapons of the world
ave divine power
nolish strongholds."

2 Cor. 10:4

What's at Stake Now

Christians today must likewise adopt a more discerning posture and a supernaturally informed wisdom, recognizing the hold that the principality of white supremacy still has in the United States. We need a political theology of the Spirit building on the best traditions of King, incorporating both a radically biblical understanding of intercessory prayer and solidarity with the poor.

Half a century after King's death, how does all this apply to today's social justice movements, such as Black Lives Matter (BLM) or Antifa, which are led by secular activists? BLM, the leading movement against police violence, has mobilized tens of thousands of young people across the country and internationally and brought much needed attention to the issue. Their work highlights the moral and political failure of the black church to speak prophetically against the use of excessive force against black people, especially in the inner city.

Yet in some ways BLM is an example of George Santayana's axiom that those who fail to learn from history are condemned to repeat it. For the most part, BLM activists – like the post-1965 SNCC activists, the Black Panther Party, and assorted other radical black groups before them – exhibit little interest in, or comprehension of, the larger lessons of history. This is because they lack the deep spiritual and moral insight that must be the grounding for any sustainable movement. Having rejected the God of their fathers, they have also rejected the fatherhood of God.

This philosophical rejection is an act of spiritual and cultural suicide. Failure to discern the demonic character of white supremacy limits these activists' ability to understand the fight they are engaged in, and hinders their efforts to develop long-term strategies. They can only describe the sadistic violence they witness and never fully understand or conquer it, so long as they ignore its spiritual source.

More importantly, they fail to use the only means of combatting the demonic: intercessory prayer. Instead, they are easily sucked into the spirit of the demonic themselves as they resort to violence, anger, and hate – a failing less common in the BLM movement than in Antifa, though the danger applies to both.

Anger and outrage cannot sustain a movement over the long term; only prayer and the power of God can. King was right to emphasize the importance of enemy-love and nonviolence. He was much more than a civil rights leader; his political philosophy was grounded in the biblical prophets and the ethics of Jesus. In the final analysis, it was the Holy Spirit, which he allowed to work in and through him, that made Martin Luther King Jr. the most influential voice of conscience and religious freedom in the United States in the twentieth century. His life and witness can continue to inspire and challenge all of us who call on the Spirit to move in our communities and across our nation. ⇝

STAYING ROOTED AND UNBALANCED

The Art of Benny Andrews

VEERY HULEATT

Born into an impoverished sharecropping family in Georgia, Benny Andrews learned to draw from his father, and then used art as a tool of survival. And not in any mystical sense: sharecropping work kept him out of school all but four or five months of the year, and he used his artistic skills to stay abreast of his studies. "I drew all the biology and plane geometry projects . . . and that, in a sense, got me through school," he told an interviewer in 1975. It also earned him a place in the School of the Art Institute of Chicago, which he attended after serving in the Korean War. Far from his native home and culture – he was one of only nine black students – Andrews struggled to stay connected to his roots. At a time when the abstract expressionism of Rothko and others was in vogue, Andrews took a realist approach, carefully portraying the people and objects of his childhood and the city around him. At the time, this was "the most subversive thing there was. . . . It almost got to the point where you were considered to be abnormal, or something was wrong with you, or you had bad breath."

His use of collage (particularly evident in *War* on page 52) was also subversive. Andrews often hung out around the institute janitors – "they were the kind of people I came from, they were like my relatives" – and wanted to paint something for them. He experimented by adding paper towels to his oil canvases to create his first collage, *Janitors at Rest.* "I didn't want to lose my sense of rawness," he said later. "Where I am

Veery Huleatt is an editor at Plough. *She lives at Fox Hill, a Bruderhof in Walden, New York.*

Benny Andrews (1930–2006), *The Long Rows,* 1966, oil on canvas, 26" x 19" / 66.0 x 48.3 cm, signed

Benny Andrews (1930–2006), *War (Study #1),* 1974, oil and graphite on canvas with painted fabric collage,
4" x 25" x 1 1/4" / 86.4 x 63.5 x 3.2 cm, signed

Benny Andrews (1930–2006), *Witness,* 1968, oil on canvas with painted fabric collage,
48" x 48" x 1" / 121.9 x 121.9 x 2.5 cm, signed

from, the people are very austere. We have big hands. We have ruddy faces. We wear rough fabrics. . . . These are my textures." In addition, the use of such unconventional materials kept him "unbalanced" as an artist. Keeping things difficult would help keep him humble and make him, in the end, the better artist.

In 1965 he began what he called his auto-biographical series – memory paintings that dealt with the lives of people he knew during his childhood in Georgia. *The Long Rows* (page 51) is an example of this, depicting his mother. Drawn from the viewpoint of a child, the painting transforms a bent woman into a heroic figure against the sky.

Benny Andrews (1930–2006), *The Way to the Promised Land (Revival Series)*, 1994, oil on canvas
with painted fabric collage, 72" x 50 3/4" x 1/4" / 182.9 x 128.9 x 0.6 cm, signed

Benny Andrews (1930–2006), *Portrait of the Black Madonna*, 1987,
oil and collage on canvas, 36″ x 48″ / 91.4 x 121.9 cm, signed

In the art world, an environment defined by prestige and money, Andrews never lost his pride in his origins and felt a responsibility to tell these stories even if it didn't earn him a welcome in galleries. He realized that it was not just himself, a black man from rural Georgia, who was excluded; other artists – women, Native Americans, prisoners, Jews, and other minorities – were also largely ignored or made to feel ashamed of their experiences and backgrounds. To Andrews, these ingredients were the foundation of artistic expression. "The problem is that there's more importance given to some people's lives, where they came from, who they are, than other people's." In the face of this disparity, he warned young artists not to assimilate in order to succeed: "If you're doing what you feel you want to do, and you're trying to enlarge upon . . . your conscience and sticking with your decisions about what you're trying to say, then that's it. That's success."

As he gained recognition, Andrews worked to diversify the art world, taught art in prisons, and, at the end of his life, launched a foundation to support young minority artists. Despite all this activism, and despite his faithful depiction of the oppressed and marginalized in his paintings, he remained modest about what art can achieve. An artist, he claimed, is simply someone with a big enough ego "to believe that if you do an apple it will convey something that the millions of people who paint apples all the time do not." But his own art – and humility – seem to belie this claim. ➤

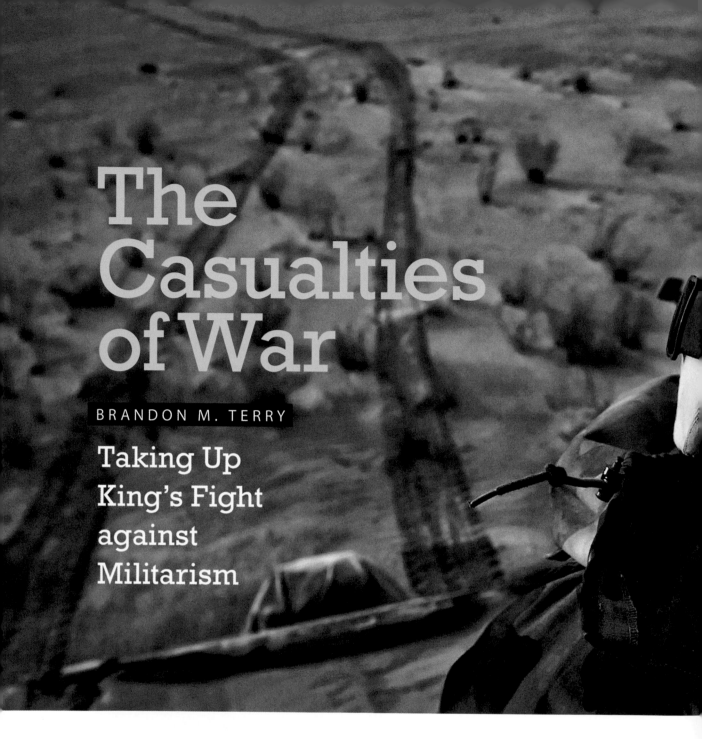

The Casualties of War

BRANDON M. TERRY

Taking Up King's Fight against Militarism

In 1967 while the Pentagon was dutifully tallying the growing count of lives and limbs lost on the killing fields of Southeast Asia, Martin Luther King Jr. joined the growing movement of Americans who began to see clearly through the fog of war. King, who since 1965 had been a relatively subtle and oblique

Brandon M. Terry is an assistant professor of African and African American studies and social studies at Harvard University.

John Partipilo, from the series *War in Iraq*

disastrous" casualties: principles and values. Today, seventeen years into the "War on Terror," King's moral clarity about war can help us face our own set of militaristic confusions.

Morality and the Budget

One of the major casualties of the war in Vietnam, King argued, was the fight against poverty. "America would never invest the necessary funds or energies in rehabilitation of its poor," King wrote, "so long as adventures like Vietnam continued to draw men and skills and money like some demonic suction tube." These words amount to what the philosopher Lionel McPherson has recently described as King's "radical call to reconsider US national priorities."

King condemned the injustice of vast numbers of Americans "perishing on

critic of the American war in Vietnam, now publicly and dramatically joined the antiwar movement. It was just a year before his tragic assassination.

It wasn't just the dead that King mourned, but also what he called the war's "equally

a lonely island of poverty in the midst of a vast ocean of material prosperity." He was especially concerned with how the misery of ghetto life overburdens African American families with intractable and unjust disadvantages: the isolation of segregated neighborhoods,

> "A nation that continues year after year to spend more money on military defense than on programs of social uplift is approaching spiritual death."
>
> Martin Luther King Jr.

the physical and psychic wounds of police misconduct, the stresses and strains of joblessness, crime, and pollution. Such enduring and expansive structural arrangements, King insisted, are an assault on dignity and self-respect, and undermine the worth of our freedoms and rights.

"What does it profit a man," he asked, "to be able to eat at an integrated lunch counter if he doesn't earn enough money to buy a hamburger and a cup of coffee?" King's moral urgency on these questions stemmed in part from his sense that the failure to secure the fair value of our rights in an affluent and ostensibly democratic society expressed a contempt that is "wasting and degrading human life." In the case of Vietnam, he asked why the vital needs of the poor did not outweigh the profligate pursuit of unjust war.

Today, our volatile mix of protracted war and entrenched poverty shows a tragic similarity to King's day. While over $600 billion is (publicly) budgeted for military expenditure, over forty million Americans live below the poverty line, with roughly nineteen million living in so-called deep poverty. Well over one million Americans survive on less than two dollars per day. Blacks remain over-represented among the US poor and unemployed, and a number of factors – including the prevalence of casual labor, the erosion of unions, and corporate consolidation in low-wage domains – mean that income has remained stubbornly slow to

rise. Worse, all such statistics are underestimates of the reality of US poverty, since they exclude the roughly 2.3 million Americans currently incarcerated.

Where poverty coincides with racial segregation and ghettoization, the obstacles to mobility are extraordinary. Take, for example, my hometown of Baltimore. The economist Raj Chetty and his colleagues have found that of the one hundred largest metro areas in the United States, Baltimore has the absolute lowest economic mobility for the poor. A poor boy growing up there, one estimate suggests, will earn about 28 percent less than he would if he had grown up somewhere *average* in America. That is, of course, if he makes it to adulthood. Baltimore has suffered over 200 homicides every year since 1990, except for one. In the last three years, homicides have reached unprecedented levels: 344 lives lost in 2015, 318 in 2016, 343 in 2017.

Yet despite the president's rhetoric of American "carnage," Congress has turned its eyes from this structural unfairness to focus primarily on increasing military funding and lowering tax rates for large corporations and the wealthy. Meanwhile, state legislatures across the country target social services for elimination and privatization by decrying their supposed wastefulness. King identified this tendency in 1967: "While the anti-poverty program is cautiously initiated, zealously supervised, and evaluated for immediate results, billions are liberally expended for this ill-considered war."

Civil Disobedience

King memorably declared that "a nation that continues year after year to spend more money on military defense than on programs of social uplift is approaching spiritual death." These words are no mere pacifist's lament, but rather

something more unsettling: King is claiming that a society marked by structural injustice and deep inequality can no longer *legitimately* command the obedience or affirmation of its most disadvantaged members. This recognition, in part, eventually led King to advocate "mass civil disobedience" against poverty and racial injustice as well as noncompliance with the Vietnam draft. Civil disobedience was, for him, about refusing – as a matter of integrity and dignity, self-respect and solidarity, democracy and justice – to cooperate willingly with such evils.

King wasn't merely reacting to abstract concerns. The controversial Moynihan Report of 1965, with its diagnosis blaming ghetto poverty primarily on a "tangle of pathology" in black families, offered among its policy prescriptions a concerted effort to recruit inner-city black males into the military, where they could learn discipline, skills, and self-esteem. This recommendation became policy with Project 100,000, a program instituted by Secretary of Defense Robert McNamara that dramatically lowered the standards of admission for the military and recruited over 300,000 formerly ineligible, disproportionately poor and minority men. These men, the military later found, were far more likely than other soldiers to be assigned to frontline combat, die in battle, and have poor life outcomes upon discharge. King indicted our reliance on such tactics as "the cruel manipulation of the poor."

In today's military, to be sure, poor and minority enlistees are no longer as overrepresented as they were in the 1970s and 1980s. The end of the draft has played a role here, as have changes to the military's recruiting standards in regards to education, physical fitness, and criminal records. But perhaps this is not the only reason for the increased proportion of white middle-class recruits. Analysts tend to explain this shift as reflecting this group's patriotism, but fail to consider that this patriotism has a dark mirror: alienation

Yuri Kozyrev, from the series *Pullout from Afghanistan*

Photograph © Yuri Kozyrev / NOOR

and dissent among minorities and the poor concerning the legitimacy of recent American wars, the persistent failure to redress racial and economic injustice, and the cynical invocation of patriotism in the face of such ills.

War Corrodes Culture

Although King focused primarily on the atrocities of war and its consequences for the poor, these weren't his only objections to militarism. Warmaking, he believed, corrodes our political culture in several ways.

Firstly, King charged that militarism is the enemy of the principles of free dissent and government accountability. He sought to defend these principles against the "ugly repressive sentiment" that wanted to "silence peace-seekers . . . as quasi-traitors, fools, or venal enemies of our soldiers and institutions."

It's a sadly contemporary warning. In fact, in some ways the Vietnam era now seems a more favorable environment for free speech and transparency than our own. Since September 11, 2001, surveillance practices that were once conducted under the cover of darkness in the FBI's Counterintelligence Program (COINTELPRO) have become standard tools of police and federal officials. Fears of terrorist attacks and uprisings have allowed police to impose absurd restrictions on public assembly. The categories of "extremist" and "terrorist" have been repurposed to surveil minority activists ("black identity extremists") and to prosecute drug dealers and gang members. A sitting US president openly exhorted NFL owners to fire players for exercising their right to free speech, and has threatened legal action against news outlets for covering government leaks. Nor is President Trump an isolated case; the Obama administration prosecuted more whistleblowers than all previous administrations combined. The chilling effect of this

antagonistic atmosphere deters many who might otherwise protest the real costs of war we usually ignore, such as civilian deaths in drone attacks, migration crises, contractor graft, and sexual assault.

Secondly, the militarist mindset tends to make our standing as citizens dependent on the prerogatives of the national security bureaucracy. This is especially pernicious for those whose equal citizenship is already vulnerable because of their race, class, national origin, or religion. Such citizens may feel a powerful temptation to swallow dissent and cast their lot with the ruling powers. A telling example of this comes from World War I, when the scholar-activist W. E. B. Du Bois called for African Americans to "forget our special grievances and close our ranks shoulder to shoulder with our own white fellow citizens." Du Bois would later come to recant this view, recognizing the sadism of this bargain. One could not think so narrowly, he would later write, that one becomes "willing to let the world go to hell, if the black man went free." As King often put it, our loyalties should become "ecumenical rather than sectional."

Defining citizenship in terms of national security reinforces the suspicion that those who persist in their dissent against war abroad and injustice at home are disloyal or internal enemies. Indeed, those are the very charges that were leveled at King when he went public with his antiwar dissent. The accusations came not just from his political opponents, but even from civil rights allies who urged him to be strategically silent for the sake of civil rights.

King would have none of it, proclaiming, "I could never again raise my voice against the violence of the oppressed in the ghettos without having first spoken clearly to the greatest purveyor of violence in the world today – my own government." For him, it was

Photograph © Yuri Kozyrev / NOOR

a matter of standing, of choosing between integrity and hypocrisy. For all who, like King, refuse to separate the rightness of means from the rightness of ends, hypocrisy is self-undermining. Their universalism is too exacting, the solidarities they generate too fragile, to bear the burdens of Machiavellian manipulation.

In our day, the costs of this hypocrisy are all too apparent. Liberal politicians, even while swathing themselves in King's legacy, wonder why their cries of moral outrage go unheeded. One reason, perhaps, that Democratic politicians get so little traction inveighing against the bigotry of the "Muslim ban" is that for eight years under the Obama administration they countenanced extralegal killings of Muslims overseas, with incinerated innocents explained away as "collateral damage."

When such mendacity becomes normal, King argues, we tragically add "cynicism to the process of death." In the Vietnam era, this cynicism took the form of a generational revolt. Our own era of endless war has spawned a less spectacular form of cynicism: widespread anomie and nihilism. We have seen, for example, a surge in heroin addiction enabled by the improbable flourishing of the opium trade in Afghanistan – the worst illicit drug epidemic in American history. Although America has spent over one trillion dollars on a continuous war in Afghanistan, the country remains ruled by an alliance of Taliban militants and drug traffickers who are, by one United Nations estimate, responsible for producing over 90 percent of the world's illegal heroin supply.

Yuri Kozyrev, from the series *Pullout from Afghanistan*

This nihilism has exacerbated racial tensions as well. Like previous movements, the recent wave of white nationalist agitation is fueled, according to the historian Kathleen Belew, by a segment of disillusioned veterans. Meanwhile, anti-Arab and anti-Islamic bigotry have become prime movers in American politics, drawing both from genuine fears of Islamic terrorist retaliation and from right-wing conspiracy theories (for example, the paranoid fear that US courts may implement shari'a law).

Even the policing controversies of the past few years have their roots in war. The story of Ferguson, Missouri, is a case in point. Media images of the 2014 clashes between police and protestors put on display the free flow of war matériel and combat personnel from foreign battlefields to local police departments. And Ferguson showed again what happens when trillions of dollars are spent on war rather than on combating poverty and enforcing fairness. In that town, an underfunded municipal government mutated into a predatory entity reliant on fees and fines forcibly extracted from vulnerable minority citizens by the police.

The American Revolutionary Tradition

For King, one of the great treasures put at risk by militarism was America's revolutionary egalitarian and democratic tradition. "The greatest irony and tragedy of all," King lamented, "is that our nation, which initiated so much of the revolutionary spirit of the modern world, is now cast in the mold of being an arch anti-revolutionary." White supremacy and imperial acquisitiveness, he argued, had misled Americans from seizing the "moral example" that might come from casting the nation's lot with "the revolution taking place in the world . . . against colonialism, reactionary dictatorship, and systems of exploitation."

In our time, however, we lack a significant antiwar movement. Opposition to war is enervated and fragile, too often satisfied with liberal anti-racism's self-righteous condemnations and charges of hypocrisy. How did we get here?

Some of the answers are simple, although no less true for being so: we are too myopic, too afraid, too distracted, and too xenophobic. Others go deeper to the rot of American democracy, in which citizenship too often becomes spectatorship and where social life – especially military service – is too often segregated by class and geography. Further, the administration of war now includes a tangled web of corporations exercising real power over our legislative and administrative bodies in search of military contracts.

Technological changes also undermine our political attention and democratic motivation. Today, war is increasingly fought on computer screens and with advanced robotics. Killing is carried out in unprecedented detachment, with too few casualties on the American side to generate sustained political outrage.

It is difficult to know what practical steps could break through the stalemate in the antiwar struggle. Yet if King's example cannot dictate what we should do *tactically*, it can teach us the *ethos* that should guide us. King's ideal of nonviolence is widely familiar. Less known and more idiosyncratic, but equally central to King's arguments against militarism, was his ideal of *maturity*.

The Virtue of Maturity

In his "Beyond Vietnam" speech at Riverside Church, King declared that "the world now demands a maturity of America that we may not be able to achieve." By maturity, King means something akin to what the philosopher Lewis Gordon has described as the ethical stance of blues music toward "the realities of adult ethical life": that "things are not always neat, that making decisions is complicated . . . that people often make mistakes," and, most importantly, that "only a child can never be guilty."

In the case of Vietnam, King argued, real maturity required that Americans, above all, accept responsibility for wrongdoing and "admit that we have been wrong from the beginning." Recognizing that our actions were "detrimental," maturity also required immediate cessation of ongoing harm and hostility, and a long-term commitment to atonement, aid, and reparation. Finally, it called for critical self-inventory and cultural correction of the passions (nationalism), ideologies (anti-Communism or racism), and drives (hypermasculinity) that have led us into a military quagmire in Afghanistan, unjust war in the Middle East, and nuclear brinksmanship in Southeast Asia.

Today the maturity King called for is essential, for "realists" no less than for everyone else. Like Gandhi, he sought to develop forms of politics and international relations that would not leave in their wake an atmosphere of bitterness, enmity, and distrust. King lamented how easily "hate multiplies hate, violence multiplies violence, and toughness multiplies toughness in a descending spiral of destruction" – and he appealed to the virtue of maturity to help break the cycle of conflict. Apology and atonement for wrongdoing are necessary as a matter of justice. Undertaken with maturity, however, they can also open the way to forgiveness and new beginnings. In Hannah Arendt's words, they can begin to "undo the deeds of the past, whose 'sins' hang like Damocles' sword over every new generation."

Such maturity – especially in the readiness to apologize and atone – should never be mistaken for the leftist tendency to substitute anti-Americanism for analysis. Nor does it seek to insulate victims of injustice from critique for their own wrongdoing: King did not flinch from criticizing revolutionaries or reactionaries abroad for their moral or political errors. All the same, he still called for Americans to "see the enemy's point of view, to hear his questions, to know his assessment of ourselves." "If we are mature," King tells us, "we may learn and grow and profit from the wisdom of the brothers who are called the opposition."

We live in a world where nuclear and biological weapons proliferate, where there are war refugees in unprecedented numbers and war profiteering in an unprecedented boom, and where far-flung and unaccountable violence begets insurgency across the globe and cynicism at home. These evils cannot be denied, and can tempt us to apathy or despair rather than humility and justice.

Yet King gives us another way of seeing. "The things that seem most real and powerful are indeed now unreal and have come under the sentence of death." Rather than continue to invoke the false idols thrown up by ideology and habit, we need "the vision to see in this generation's ordeals the opportunity to transfigure both ourselves and American society." With maturity, we must once again learn to see the real casualties of war amidst the fog, and then act. ➤

> "If we are mature we may learn and grow and profit from the wisdom of the brothers who are called the opposition."
>
> Martin Luther King Jr.

Photograph by Yoichi Okamoto, Wikimedia Commons (public domain)

Why I Oppose War

I sometimes marvel at those who ask me why
    I am speaking against the war.
Could it be that they do not know
    that the Good News was meant for all men –
        for communist and capitalist,
        for their children and ours,
        for black and for white,
        for revolutionary and conservative?
Have they forgotten that my ministry is in obedience to the one
    who loved his enemies so fully
        that he died for them? . . .

I must be true to my conviction that I share with all men
    the calling to be a son of the living God.
Beyond the calling of race or nation or creed
    is this vocation of sonship and brotherhood. . . .

We are called to speak for the weak, for the voiceless,
    for victims of our nation and for those it calls enemy,
for no document from human hands
    can make these humans any less our brothers.

Source: Martin Luther King Jr., "Beyond Vietnam: A Time to Break Silence," speech at Riverside Church in New York City, April 4, 1967.

Zoe Cromwell, *Untitled,* acrylic on canvas, 2013

"Gaza is not far away." —*Dr. Luke Peterson*

It's in your cuffs.
The cup you just drank from.
Empty bucket outside your back door with an inch of rain in it.
Sack of mulch to scatter on your winter beds.
Do you see these things as luxury?
It's the crosswalk kids march in.
Mama with her yellow belt
waving them through. It's rules.
It's everything you keep a long time
in your refrigerator – pickles, tonic, apple butter.
Butter. The fact you have a refrigerator
and power to run it all day long.
Gaza might like that.

NAOMI SHIHAB NYE

"I can never be what I ought to be until you are what you ought to be."
Martin Luther King Jr.

D. L. MAYFIELD

For the Love of Neighbor

A 108-year-old Bhutanese refugee in Austin, Texas

"When Grandma was ten, Martin Luther King Jr. was killed." My seven-year-old daughter likes to bring up this fact at random times. It startles me, her easy connection to a death five decades ago. I never told her this, exactly. I did read her a book about Ruby Bridges, the first black girl to integrate an all-white school in 1960, noting that Bridges, who is alive and well, is the exact same age as my mother. When my daughter learned about King during Black History Month at her school last year, she must have remembered this detail and fused the dates, linking King to the beloved grandmother whose life is her lens into history.

My own memories of learning about Martin Luther King Jr. are hazier. I remember being

told, when I was very young, that he was an adulterer. I remember absorbing the belief from my school books that he was a man who helped to end racism in my country a long, long time ago. And in college, at a Bible school, I remember analyzing his "Letter from a Birmingham Jail" as a masterpiece of rhetoric, with little attention paid to the content or to the awareness that I and my tribe might fit into the exact audience to whom King was writing. I was disconnected both from the power of his faith-fueled nonviolent action and to the immediacy of his words to our present context.

Yet the older I get, the more deeply I find myself moved by this man, especially his bedrock belief in neighbor-love. "Love your neighbor" – the words sound so simplistic, yet coming from a man who practiced them at great cost to himself, they are no mere

---

D. L. Mayfield works with refugee communities and is the author of Assimilate or Go Home: Notes from a Failed Missionary on Rediscovering Faith *(HarperOne, 2016). She lives in Portland, Oregon, with her husband and two children.*

Bhutanese refugees using a food stamp card at a grocery store in Austin, Texas

platitude. What does it take to truly love your neighbor? In answering that question, King turned the parable of the Good Samaritan on its head, calling Christians to more than mere acts of charity. He said, "We must come to see that the whole Jericho Road must be transformed so that men and women will not be constantly beaten and robbed as they make their journey on life's highway." The Christian, King says, not only takes care of those in trouble but looks to the systems actively oppressing them.

A Modern-Day Jericho Road

We need such an interpretation again today, shouted from the rooftops by people who have spent their life's work both tending to the beaten and demanding that the Jericho Road become a place of safety. While King spoke primarily about poverty in the United States, surely there is no limit to the geography of neighbor-love. As the world has become increasingly connected by trade, war, migration, and social media, our responsibility to our global neighbor has grown too.

Yet that's not the way many of my fellow believers see it. American Christians – or, to be more precise, white evangelical Christians – are now world-famous for their overwhelming support for building a wall between the United States and Mexico and deporting the undocumented people who are already here. These attitudes form part of a broader picture: 76 percent of white evangelicals approve of Trump's travel ban on Muslims, and 69 percent are "very concerned" about domestic Islamic extremism (only a third of non-religious Americans feel the same way). My people – the ones who raised me to go and be a light and a witness for Christ among the nations – are more likely than any other Christian group to say they have low respect for Muslims.

What would Martin Luther King Jr. say to people who claim to follow God while spearheading a movement aimed at closing borders, building walls, separating families, and cold-shouldering the persecuted and destitute? His words seem as relevant as ever: "One of the great tragedies of man's long trek along the highway of history has been the limiting of neighborly concern to tribe, race, class, or nation."

The Other America

I'll admit that King's convictions on this point did not make sense to me either until I experienced firsthand what the effects of our still-segregated society are. In my early twenties, I found myself working with refugee families in my city of Portland, Oregon. I became sucked into their lives on the periphery of my glowing, busy city: the dingy apartment complexes with predatory landlords, the under-resourced and understaffed schools, the endless tangles of bureaucracy in order to get basic needs met. The more I hung out in refugee communities, the more I saw "the Other America" that King spoke about: the America that lives in poverty and economic despair.

> "If the church does not recapture its prophetic zeal, it will become an irrelevant social club without moral or spiritual authority."
>
> Martin Luther King Jr.

Getting to know refugees also brought me into contact with others who were disproportionately affected by poverty. I started to second-guess what I had absorbed about the American Dream: that anyone could make something of themselves if only they tried hard enough. I learned how segregated our school systems are, how segregated our cities are (on purpose, through practices like redlining), and how the criminal justice system disproportionately targets and incarcerates communities of color. I met so many people who had been left by the wayside of the Jericho Road.

Story by story, neighbor by neighbor, I began to see. Refugees, immigrants, black men and Native American women, families suffering under generational poverty – they all became my teachers. Over time I began to understand the systemic nature of their experiences, and my own role and responsibility to bear witness.

I know how the recent travel bans have devastated lives, because I know people for whom the bans are personal: families who have survived hell on earth and who have beat insurmountable odds to resettle in the United States (where less than 1 percent of all refugees end up) – only to realize that their dreams of being reunited with family members are now on hold indefinitely. Last year one young woman showed me pictures of her fiancé, who lives and works in Germany, giggling as she talked about her hopes for their life together. Now she is caught in an impossible dilemma: since her fiancé is a national of a country currently on the US travel ban list, there is little to no possibility he will be able to join her. Does she stay here with her siblings and mother and father (who is paralyzed due to a sniper's bullet), or does she say goodbye in order to be with the man she loves?

Another friend of mine, who has lived in the United States for almost two years, tells me she has been sleeping too much during the day. Her arms hurt and she has dark shadows under her eyes. When I ask what is wrong, she shows me pictures of her elderly mother, in her eighties, lying very sick in a hospital across the world. My friend cannot leave America to visit her until she gets US citizenship, which takes five years of residency to attain. Nor will our country give her mother a travel visa. My friend feels trapped, stuck in her apartment, cooking food for her children and her neighbors, going to English class, fighting to start over – all the while mourning the reality that she will not be able to say goodbye to her mother in person.

I sit in my friends' apartments; they serve me food and try to smile. Then I go home and

see Facebook posts from Christian friends and family members gleeful about building border walls and banning entire nations from immigrating based on religion. How can all this energy and passion be spent on drawing lines between which people do and do not belong? Without my neighbors and their stories of anguish and hope, I would never recognize the Jericho Road conditions in my own country. For that, I am grateful. And heartbroken.

A Burning House?

According to the United Nations, in 2016 over 65.2 million people, more than half of them children, were forcibly displaced as a result of violence, conflict, persecution, or lack of human rights. Despite the horror that these statistics represent, the United States is on track to resettle less than half of the lowest proposed number of refugee cases in the history of the refugee resettlement program. This program was created after World War II in part to atone for past sins such as denying visas to Jews looking to escape the Holocaust. Now, as the program dwindles, I fear that we as a country will have to atone for our omission in the eyes of a just and loving God.

The day before he was assassinated, King phoned his church and gave them the title of his sermon: "Why America May Go to Hell." While we can never know what exactly he planned to preach, the title strikes me as sadly relevant to the American church in 2018. As King so eloquently said, "If the church does not recapture its prophetic zeal, it will become an irrelevant social club without moral or spiritual authority. If the church does not actively participate in the struggle for peace and for economic and racial justice, it will forfeit the loyalty of millions and cause men everywhere to say that it has atrophied its will."

Through my work with refugee families, I have been pushed to the limits of compassion and challenged to think about my own role and the role of my community in creating such a broken Jericho Road. I can reach out and touch it with my fingers – the ways my religion and my country have added to the violence in the world. America is built on empire, said King, but Jesus built on love. We have a lot more building to do.

King spent the last years of his life building coalitions between sometimes unlikely groups in the pursuit of a moral revival focused on

A resident of Austin, Texas, shares a meal with Bhutanese friends.

the issues affecting the poor: black, white, and immigrant: "I think it is necessary for us to realize that we have moved from the era of civil rights to the era of human rights . . . when we see that there must be a radical redistribution of economic and political power." While today's global refugee crisis was not a challenge he faced, it's clear where his sympathies lay: he worked with migrants in the United States and even sent Cesar Chavez a telegram saying that their "separate struggles are really one."

In his "Letter from a Birmingham Jail," King wrote about giving thanks that "noble souls from the ranks of organized religion have broken loose from the paralyzing chains of conformity and joined us as active partners in the struggle for freedom," calling these Christians who risked offending the status quo "the spiritual salt that has preserved the true meaning of the gospel in these troubled times." But right up to the end of his life, he struggled with the chasm between the stated values of American Christians and how they actually lived and loved their neighbors. "Are we integrating into a burning house?" he asked himself and others. Sometimes I am tempted to ask the same question. As I ask my fellow Christians to welcome immigrants and refugees, to take care of the sojourner and the widow and the orphan, I long for a new understanding of hospitality in our nation, starting from within our churches.

Loving Tomorrow's Neighbors

When I was my daughter's age I wanted to be a missionary. I wanted to do big things for God, and this seemed like the grandest gesture one could make: to leave your family behind, sail off into another world, and save everyone. My life took a few twists and turns, but when I was

twenty I found myself in a foreign country for a few months, testing the waters to see if I could make it for the long haul. I loved the experience of being a foreigner – the new food, the new culture, the excitement of difference – but sometimes I would be shocked. Like when one of my beloved hosts made an offhand and derogatory comment about the Roma ("gypsies") in her city. I protested that it was wrong to put down an entire group of people. My host looked at me calmly and asked, "But what about the way you white Americans treated black people?" I was stunned silent.

This kind of learning, while painful, is vital. Some days I'm undone by the changes that refuse to happen, by the daily impossibilities my nearest neighbors face just to get through each day.

I am learning, too, not to be afraid of owning my piece in the story of violence and inhospitality. If the American church stands idly by while our nation closes its doors to the most vulnerable of God's children, we might well be on our way to becoming that irrelevant country club.

And yet, as I look at my daughter, at the children she goes to school with, the books she reads, and how she makes sense of the world, I have hope. I pray that as she connects the dots – between herself and Martin Luther King, between pioneers like Ruby Bridges and her friends from Somalia, Mexico, and Syria – these connections will continue to build her capacity to love her neighbor, even in the midst of fearful times.

And I have faith in a God who saves us from our sins, the God who wants to redeem everyone: the beaten and battered on life's highway, the Levites and priests who ignore them, and all of us who are caught up in the structure of suffering and guilt that is the Jericho Road. ✍

Photograph by Matt Herron / AP Images

Now Is the Time

We are now faced with the fact that tomorrow is today.
We are confronted with the fierce urgency of now.

In this unfolding conundrum of life and history
    there is such a thing as being too late. . . .
There is an invisible book of life that faithfully records
    our vigilance or our neglect. . . .

Now let us begin. Now let us rededicate ourselves
    to the long and bitter – but beautiful – struggle for a new world.
This is the calling of the sons of God,
    and our brothers wait eagerly for our response.

Shall we say the odds are too great? Shall we tell them
    the struggle is too hard?
Will our message be that the forces of American life
    militate against their arrival as full men,
        and we send our deepest regrets?
Or will there be another message,
    of longing, of hope, of solidarity with their yearnings,
        of commitment to their cause, whatever the cost? ⇒

Source: Martin Luthe King Jr., "Beyond Vietnam: A Time to Break Silence," speech at Riverside Church in New York City, April 4, 1967.

Two Friends Two Prophets

Abraham Joshua Heschel and Martin Luther King Jr.

SUSANNAH HESCHEL

"RACISM IS SATANISM." It was this conviction that launched Rabbi Abraham Joshua Heschel, a religious Jew from a Hasidic family in Poland, into the American civil rights movement.

He appears beside Martin Luther King Jr. in several of the most iconic photographs of that time: crossing Edmund Pettus Bridge arm in arm in March 1965; standing together outside Arlington Cemetery in silent protest of the Vietnam War in 1968.

We've become so used to these images that it's easy to forget how unusual the friendship between Heschel and King was in its day. The two came from very different backgrounds – King had grown up in Atlanta, Georgia, while Heschel arrived in the United States as a refugee from Hitler's Europe in March of 1940 – "a brand plucked from the fire," as he wrote. Yet the two found an intimacy that transcended the growing public rift between their two communities. Heschel brought King and his message to a wide Jewish audience,

Heschel and King at Arlington National Cemetery, February 6, 1968

Susannah Heschel is an author and professor of Jewish studies at Dartmouth College. She is the daughter of Abraham Joshua Heschel.

Photograph by John C. Goodwin

and King made Heschel a central figure in the struggle for civil rights. Often lecturing together, they both spoke about racism as the root of poverty and its role in the war in Vietnam; both also spoke about Zionism and about the struggles of Jews in the Soviet Union. The concern that they shared was "saving the soul of America."

KING AND HESCHEL first met in Chicago at the 1963 conference on "Religion and Race" organized by the National Conference of Christians and Jews (NCCJ). The bond between them was immediate. King's speech at the conference, "A Challenge to the Churches and Synagogues," affirmed that the struggle against racism was an interfaith effort:

> The churches and synagogues have an opportunity and a duty to lift up their voices like a trumpet and declare unto the people the immorality of segregation. We must affirm that every human life is a reflex of divinity, and every act of injustice mars and defaces the image of God in man. The undergirding philosophy of segregation is diametrically opposed to the undergirding philosophy of our Judeo-Christian heritage, and all the dialectics of the logicians cannot make them lie down together.

"Every act of injustice mars and defaces the image of God in man."
Martin Luther King Jr.

Heschel followed King, opening his speech by bringing his audience into a dramatic biblical narrative:

> At the first conference on religion and race, the main participants were Pharaoh and Moses. . . . The outcome of that summit meeting has not come to an end. Pharaoh is not ready to capitulate. The exodus began, but is far from having been completed. In fact, it was easier for the children of Israel to cross the Red Sea than for a Negro to cross certain university campuses.

Heschel's passionate speech electrified the audience – Cornel West has called it the strongest condemnation of racism by a white man since William Lloyd Garrison. "Racism is Satanism, unmitigated evil," Heschel declared. "You cannot worship God and at the same time look at man as if he were a horse." Religion cannot coexist with racism: it is a grave violation of the fundamental religious principle not to murder. Racism is public humiliation, which is condemned in the Talmud as tantamount to murder: "One should rather commit suicide than offend a person publicly."

His critique extended to religious communities: "We worry more about the purity of dogma than about the integrity of love. . . . What is lacking is a sense of the monstrosity of inequality." Racism is "the test of our integrity, a magnificent spiritual opportunity" for radical change. "Reverence for God is shown in reverence for man. . . . To be arrogant toward man is to be blasphemous toward God."

HESCHEL AND KING shared a disdain for the popular liberal Protestant theology of the era, and a skepticism for orthodoxies. They mocked Paul Tillich's definition of God as the "ground of being," helpless in the face of injustice. Both thought that Karl Barth's theology left "the average mind lost in the fog of theological abstractions," as King wrote.

In response to this religious impotence, Heschel created a new theological approach that, like King's, combined a conservative theology with a liberal politics. His book *The Prophets*, a major expansion of his German doctoral dissertation, first appeared in English in 1962. During the years Heschel was preparing it, he was attentive to King's activities and the civil rights movement, and his book reflects the political passions of the era.

When the book was published, it gained enormous attention among Bible scholars and theologians as a multifaceted and groundbreaking work. Heschel delivered a devastating critique of Protestant biblical scholarship, developed new criteria for interpreting the prophetic texts, and brought to the fore a neglected but central Jewish theological tradition of understanding God, revelation, and the human.

But his work didn't stay in the libraries of academia. Andrew Young, James Lawson, Vincent Harding, C. T. Vivian, and Bayard Rustin were among the young activists in the nonviolence movement who told me they carried a copy of the paperback edition in their back pocket for inspiration and consolation.

B Y THE TIME Heschel and King met, the nation was tense: the Birmingham campaign was underway in the first months of 1963, and on June 11, 1963, George Wallace, governor of Alabama, attempted to block the enrollment of Vivian Malone and James Hood at the University of Alabama; federal troops forced him to step aside. That night, President Kennedy delivered a major televised speech, promising legislation and calling civil rights a "moral issue." The next day, Medgar Evers, field secretary of the NAACP in Mississippi, was murdered.

King was preparing that summer of 1963 for the March on Washington for Jobs and Freedom, organized by A. Philip Randolph and Bayard Rustin, a demonstration President Kennedy hoped to avert. Kennedy invited a group of civil rights leaders, including Heschel, to the White House for a meeting on June 20. Heschel replied to the invitation with a telegram dated June 16:

> Please demand of religious leaders personal involvement not just solemn declaration. We forfeit right to worship God as long as we continue to humiliate Negroes. Church synagogue have failed, they must repent. Ask of religious leaders to call for national repentance and personal sacrifice. Let religious leaders donate one month's salary toward fund for Negro housing and education. I propose that you Mr. President declare state of moral emergency. . . . The hour calls for moral grandeur and spiritual audacity.

"The hour calls for moral grandeur and spiritual audacity."
Abraham Joshua Heschel

The March on Washington took place in August 1963, with more than two hundred thousand people participating.

Their pleas were met by a disappointing silence. President Kennedy did not declare a state of moral emergency, nor did clergy donate a month of salary to housing and education. If anything, the tensions in the United States grew even more dire. Just weeks later, on September 15, 1963, a church in Birmingham was bombed, killing four young black girls. That same day, James Bevel and Diane Nash launched the Alabama Project that ultimately led to the famous march from Selma to Montgomery in 1965.

Barry Moser, *The Prophet Jeremiah*, relief engraving, 1998–1999

"For if you truly amend *your ways and your doings, if you truly execute justice one with another, if you do not oppress the alien, the fatherless or the widow, or shed innocent blood . . . then I will let you dwell in this place, in the land that I gave of old to your fathers forever."*

—*Jeremiah 7:5*

THE PROPHETS – both Heschel's book and the biblical figures – drew Heschel and King together. Both men were trained theologians who also knew how to preach. King was the organizer and public figure, while Heschel was the theologian and scholar with the voice of a public intellectual. Prophetic rhetoric has a long public history in the United States, yet it was not only the prophets' words that stood out. For King and Heschel, the prophets were extraordinary human beings with passionate emotional lives, people who knew how to pray and who created powerful symbolic moments.

Both believed too that the passions of the prophets reflect the passion of God. As Heschel saw it, we learn from the prophets that the God of the Hebrew Bible is a God of pathos who responds with passion to human actions: "With Israel's distress came the affliction of God." Divine pathos is matched by prophetic sympathy, the prophet's ability to resonate to God's inner life.

Not only did King integrate verses from the prophetic books of the Bible into his speeches, he also transferred the current moment into biblical time. He spoke of himself as Moses on the mountaintop. In a less renowned speech, he likened civil rights activists to the burning bush: "Bull Connor next would say, 'Turn the fire hoses on.' And as I said to you the other night Bull Connor didn't know history. He knew a kind of physics that somehow didn't relate to the transphysics that we knew about, and that was the fact that there was a certain kind of fire that no water could put out."

Heschel spoke in similar terms in his 1964 speech, "The White Man on Trial":

The tragedy of Pharaoh was the failure to realize that the exodus from slavery could have spelled redemption for both Israel and Egypt. Would that Pharaoh and the Egyptians had joined the Israelites in the desert and together stood at the foot of Sinai!

The prophet reminds his listeners of their moral obligation to respond, not simply to the prophet, but to those who suffer as a consequence of our immoral society. In this sense King's "beloved community" is a moral invitation to choose citizenship in an alternative community of nonviolence seeking to overcome what King identified as the three evils of poverty, racism, and militarism.

A NEW DIMENSION of prophecy was introduced through the civil rights movement: the prophecy of body and action. What generated the power of the movement was not only the prophetic rhetoric, rooted in the preaching of the black Christian tradition and in the classic American jeremiad, but also the use of the body, responding to violence with nonviolence. The body became the symbolic representation of prophecy. Susie Linfield concludes her book, *The Cruel Radiance: Photography and Political Violence,* with a question posed by photographer Gilles Peress: "How do you make the unseen seen?" The presence of the nonviolent body, sitting or marching, made the teachings visible.

Moreover, the passion of the prophets made their inner religious lives palpable. For Heschel, a pillar of authentic prophecy was the prophet's ability to hold God and man in one thought at one time. About Jeremiah, for example, Heschel wrote, "Standing before the people he pleaded for God; standing before God he pleaded for his people." The prophet stands within the state, but apart from state power.

Similarly, the civil rights movement needed to challenge and overturn the state's understanding of the human. What Heschel called the "eye disease" of racism, which had excluded black Americans from the civic state, had placed itself outside the civic bond of moral justice. Such statements are not rhetoric alone, but make a claim upon the listeners: prophecy is a demand, not a comfort or reassurance. It demands action.

THE 1965 MARCH from Selma to Montgomery was a major event for both Heschel and King. A few days before the march took place, Heschel led a delegation of eight hundred people to FBI headquarters in New York City in order to protest the brutal treatment of demonstrators in Selma. On Friday, March 19, two days before the Selma march was scheduled to begin, Heschel received a telegram from King, inviting him to join the marchers. Heschel was welcomed as one of the leaders in the front row of marchers, with King, Ralph Bunche, and Ralph Abernathy. Each of them wore flower leis brought by Hawaiian delegates. In an unpublished memoir that he wrote upon returning from Selma, Heschel describes the extreme hostility he encountered from whites in Alabama from the moment he arrived at the airport, in contrast to the kindness he was shown by King's assistants.

King's "beloved community" is an invitation to choose citizenship in an alternative community of nonviolence.

Heschel's presence in the front row of marchers was a visual symbol of religious Jewish commitment to civil rights, and "stirred not only the Jewish religious community but Jews young and old into direct action, galvanizing the whole spectrum of activists from fundraisers to lawyers." Not everyone reacted as positively to the marchers; the *New York Times* carried a report that Republican Representative William L. Dickinson had called the march a Communist plot, claiming that "drunkenness and sex orgies were the order of the day."

Upon his return home, Heschel described his experience in a diary entry:

> I felt a sense of the holy in what I was doing. Dr. King expressed several times to me his appreciation. He said, "I cannot tell you how much your presence means to us. You cannot imagine how often Reverend [C. T.] Vivian and I speak about you." Dr. King said to me that this was the greatest day in his life and the most important civil rights demonstration. . . . I felt again what I have been thinking about for years – that Jewish religious institutions have again missed a great opportunity, namely, to interpret a civil rights movement in terms of Judaism. The vast majority of Jews participating actively in it are totally unaware of what the movement means in terms of the prophetic traditions.

"I felt my legs were praying," Heschel said. The march reminded him of walking with Hasidic rebbes, an experience of prayer in the world of Hasidic piety. Hasidism sought to endow all physical acts with the presence of the soul. To walk with a rebbe meant to experience the holy in everyday actions, to feel the divine radiance emanating from him, and recognize that walking, too, can be directed to heaven as prayer.

WHETHER OR NOT King should speak out publicly against the war in Vietnam was a topic that preoccupied Heschel during the years between 1965 and

Barry Moser, *Hosea and Gomer*, relief engraving, 1998–1999

"In that day . . . *I will abolish the bow, the sword, and war from the land; and I will make you lie down in safety. And I will betroth you to me forever; I will betroth you to me in righteousness and in justice, in steadfast love, and in mercy."* —*Hosea 2:15–19*

1967. Would King's public opposition to the war hurt the civil rights movement? Which was the better political course, and which was the greater moral good? Lacking widespread support for a public position against the war even within the Southern Christian Leadership Conference which he led, King came under severe attack for his opposition. Civil

Barry Moser, *The Prophet Amos,* relief engraving, 1998–1999

"Because you trample upon the poor *and take from him exactions of wheat, you have built houses of hewn stone, but you shall not dwell in them. . . .*

"For I know how many are your transgressions, and how great are your sins – you who afflict the righteous, who take a bribe, and turn aside the needy in the gate." —Amos 5:11–12

rights leaders including Ralph Bunche, Roy Wilkins, Jackie Robinson, and Senator Edward Brooke publicly criticized him, and major newspapers within both the black and white communities editorialized against him. King was attacked for potentially undermining President Lyndon Johnson's support for the civil rights movement. Urban League director Whitney Young even argued that "the greatest freedom that exists for Negroes . . . is the freedom to die in Vietnam."

Against this background, King delivered his address against the war in Vietnam, one of his most important speeches, on April 4, 1967, to an enormous audience at Riverside Church in New York City, at a gathering organized by Clergy and Laymen Concerned about Vietnam (CALCAV). Heschel introduced him, saying:

Our thoughts on Vietnam are sores, destroying our trust, ruining our most cherished commitments with burdens of shame. We are pierced to the core with pain, and it is our duty as citizens to say no to the subversiveness of our government, which is ruining the values we cherish. . . . The blood we shed in Vietnam makes a mockery of all our proclamations, dedications, celebrations. Has our conscience become a fossil, is all mercy gone? If mercy, the mother of humility, is still alive as a demand, how can we say yes to our bringing agony to that tormented country? We are here because our own integrity as human beings is decaying in the agony and merciless killing done in our name. In a free society, some are guilty and all are responsible. We are here to call upon the governments of the United States as well as North Vietnam to stand still and to consider that no victory is worth the price of terror, which all parties commit in Vietnam, North and South. Remember that the blood of the innocent cries forever. Should that blood stop to cry, humanity would cease to be.

Echoing Heschel, King reminded his audience of the SCLC's motto, "To save the soul of America," and added, "If America's soul becomes totally poisoned, part of the autopsy must read Vietnam. . . . A nation that continues year after year to spend more money on military defense than on programs of social uplift is approaching spiritual death." He went on to call for a "revolution of values" in American society as the best defense against communism, and "to remove those conditions of poverty, insecurity, and injustice which are the fertile soil in which the seed of communism grows and develops."

These were prophetic speeches that led to prophetic action. A few months later, CALCAV requested permission to hold a demonstration against the war at Arlington National Cemetery. Permission for a demonstration was denied, but a prayer service was permitted, with each person limited to one sentence. The event was held on February 6, 1968. The following month, on March 25, 1968, just ten days before he was assassinated, King returned to a hotel in the Catskills to deliver the keynote address at a birthday celebration honoring Heschel, convened by the Rabbinical Assembly of America, an umbrella organization of Conservative rabbis. This was their final meeting.

> "In a free society, some are guilty and all are responsible."
> *Abraham Joshua Heschel*

ERE HESCHEL AND King the prophets of America? Neither claimed the title, but each spoke of the other as a prophet. In introducing King to the audience, Heschel asked, "Where in America today do we hear a voice like the voice of the prophets of Israel? Martin Luther King is a sign that God has not forsaken the United States of America. God has sent him to us. His presence is the hope of America. His mission is sacred, his leadership of supreme importance to every one of us."

In response, King stated that Heschel "is indeed a truly great prophet. . . . Here and there we find those who refuse to remain silent behind the safe security of stained glass windows, and they are forever seeking to make the great ethical insights of our Judeo-Christian heritage relevant in this day and in this age." ⤙

Robert Frost's "Birches"

SO WAS I ONCE MYSELF A SWINGER OF BIRCHES.

AND SO I DREAM OF GOING BACK TO BE.

IT'S WHEN I'M WEARY OF CONSIDERATIONS, AND LIFE IS TOO MUCH LIKE A PATHLESS WOOD

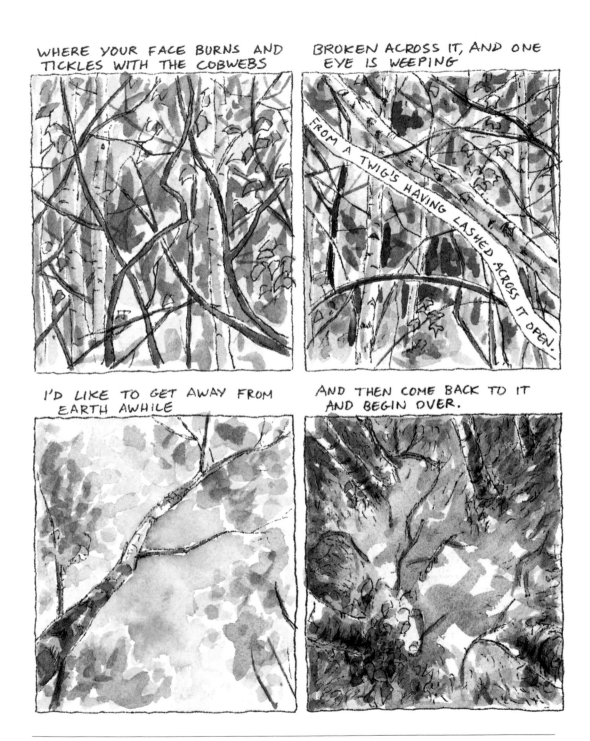

WHERE YOUR FACE BURNS AND TICKLES WITH THE COBWEBS

BROKEN ACROSS IT, AND ONE EYE IS WEEPING

FROM A TWIG'S HAVING LASHED ACROSS IT OPEN.

I'D LIKE TO GET AWAY FROM EARTH AWHILE

AND THEN COME BACK TO IT AND BEGIN OVER.

Julian Peters is an illustrator and comic book artist living in Montreal, Canada, who focuses on adapting classical poems into graphic art. His work has been exhibited internationally and published in several poetry and graphic art collections. julianpeterscomics.com

MAY NO FATE WILLFULLY MISUNDERSTAND ME
AND HALF GRANT WHAT I WISH AND SNATCH ME AWAY

NOT TO RETURN. EARTH'S THE RIGHT PLACE FOR LOVE:
I DON'T KNOW WHERE IT'S LIKELY TO GO BETTER.

I'D LIKE TO GO BY CLIMBING A BIRCH TREE,

AND CLIMB BLACK BRANCHES UP A SNOW-WHITE TRUNK

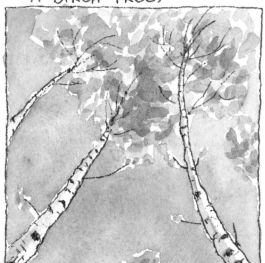

TOWARD HEAVEN, TILL THE TREE COULD BEAR NO MORE,

BUT DIPPED ITS TOP

AND SET ME DOWN AGAIN.

THAT WOULD BE GOOD BOTH GOING AND COMING BACK.

ONE COULD DO WORSE THAN BE A SWINGER OF BIRCHES.

THE END

Editors' Picks

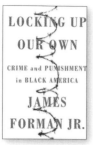

Locking Up Our Own
James Forman Jr.
(Farrar, Straus and Giroux)

Mass incarceration, particularly of young black males, is now front and center of the struggle for racial justice and civil rights, thanks in part to Michelle Alexander's 2010 book, *The New Jim Crow*. Forman, a Yale Law School professor, adds nuance to our understanding of why the US prison population has grown fivefold over the last four decades, with 2.3 million incarcerated today. He doesn't deny the role of racism, but shows how black leaders and citizens, faced with an explosion of crime in their communities during the crack epidemic, also came to support aggressive policing and harsh sentencing.

As a public defender in Washington, DC, Forman often found himself in courtrooms where not only was the defendant black; the victim, judge, prosecutor, defense attorney, court reporter, and bailiff were as well. So were the policeman who made the arrest, the city councilors who wrote the laws, the police chief, the mayor, and the prison guards. Forman particularly came to hate judges' "Martin Luther King speech" to young offenders before sending them off to prison: "Dr. King didn't march and die so that . . . you could be out on the street, getting high, carrying a gun, and robbing people."

It's the personal stories that stay with you. A young woman, one of the few in her neighborhood to secure a decent job, is arrested for possession of marijuana after being pulled over in a traffic stop. Though the charges are dropped, she is fired and unable to find work because of her arrest record. In a more hopeful example, the only thing that saves a (poor, black) juvenile from a life in the criminal justice system after an armed robbery is his (poor, black) victim's willingness to forgive him and support his bid for a second chance in a vocational program.

A final chapter offers a word of caution: would-be reformers of the US criminal justice system have often invoked a convenient distinction between "nonviolent drug offenders" (deemed worthy of leniency) and everyone else in prison ("violent criminals" who "belong in cages"). Yet nonviolent drug offenders only make up 10 percent of the prison population. Even if all were released tomorrow, the horror of mass incarceration would still be with us. What might a justice system look like that rehabilitates as effectively as it now punishes, and that leaves room for mercy?

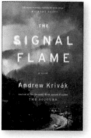

The Signal Flame
Andrew Krivák
(Scribner)

Every generation has its war. And every war casts a long shadow back home in the mountains of Pennsylvania.

Two absent characters make their presence felt throughout this novel: recently buried family patriarch Josef Vinich, and young Sam Konar, last seen in Vietnam. Those left to carry on have more than their share of loss. It's no surprise they struggle with a God who, like the author, seems to create beautiful characters only to kill them off in the next chapter, or worse, leave them missing in action, their loved ones suspended between hope and grief.

The rains fall equally on deserving and undeserving, and as the waters keep rising, one wonders if the gray will ever lift. But it does. And those left standing find healing together, thanks to another invisible actor that Krivák would probably call grace – the only force that can make two feuding families one.

The book is steeped in biblical metaphor, but rendered as naturally as his understated depictions of wooded ridges and trout streams, sawmills and well-built homes. To find a new literary writer who knows how faith shapes the stories of our lives and times is downright refreshing.

Meetings with Remarkable Manuscripts
Christopher de Hamel
(Penguin)

Readers who appreciate a well-designed book will love this one, which unravels the stories behind some of history's most valuable documents. The handsome volume, which has won the Wolfson History Prize and the Duff Cooper Prize, is a work of art in its own right, with over 200 full-color illustrations in a 640-page hardcover.

A Cambridge historian and former Sotheby's expert, de Hamel is a qualified guide. His entertaining and informative introduction to twelve manuscripts created between the sixth and sixteenth centuries opens a window into the medieval world. He also takes the reader along on his travels to "meet" each manuscript, offering running commentary of his experiences in today's high-stakes world of rare books.

Few might think this topic thrilling or newsworthy, but passion is contagious. Shortly after the release of this book, de Hamel announced he had discovered Thomas Becket's own copy of the Psalms, which he may well have been holding when he was martyred in Canterbury

Cathedral back in 1170. In other news, Italy has agreed to loan the *Codex Amiatinus* – an illuminated Bible, 2,080 pages long and the oldest surviving copy of the Vulgate – back to Britain 1,302 years after it left English shores.

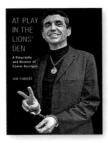

At Play in the Lions' Den
Jim Forest
(Orbis)

Amid the wealth of biographies published lately, you'll be hard pressed to find another as spirited as Forest's intimate look at the life and faith of his friend Daniel Berrigan (1921–2016) and a colorful cast of friends and associates that includes Thomas Merton, Dorothy Day, Thich Nhat Hanh, Martin Luther King Jr., Ernesto Cardenal, and Martin Sheen.

Celebrated as a rebel priest, poet, activist, and teacher, Berrigan was famous enough in his day to make the cover of *Time*. But even his own religious community didn't always appreciate him. And the strength of his personal beliefs was tested not only by stints in prison for civil disobedience but also by the zeitgeist. Fun-loving and generous he may have been, but he also took confession – and forgiveness – of sins seriously. He never wavered in his views that a vow made before God ought to be upheld, that violence can never be redemptive, and that every life is sacred.

Packed with vivid anecdotes, photographs, and quotes from Berrigan's many books, Forest's profile aptly illustrates why his fascinating subject chose the following epitaph for his gravestone: "It was never dull. Alleluia!"
—➤ *The Editors*

Marc Chagall, *The Lovers,* oil on canvas, 1920

Defending Purity

Reading Dietrich von Hildebrand in a #MeToo Age

NATHANIEL PETERS

My senior year of college I lived on a floor with gender-neutral bathrooms. One evening I came in with my toothbrush to find a friend from down the hall standing in front of the mirror. She had come from a conservative evangelical family and was now a feminist majoring in sociology. But that night she stood there in hurt astonishment, repeating to herself, "How did I become so cheap?"

American young people have come of age in a time when the ideals of the sexual revolution are unquestioned gospel truths. On the one hand, the sexual revolution taught us that the physical and emotional pleasures of sex are the highest goods in life. On the other hand, it taught us that sex is not sacred, but simply a natural urge, like our desires for water and food. People in my generation are beginning to see the cost of these precepts, especially for women.

Young people like my friend need to know how to love and be loved in a way that acknowledges their great value, and Christians are called to show them a more excellent way. This can be done by example, of course, but we also have the aid of thinkers who help us to articulate the dignity of each person and the sanctity of sex.

Some of the most successful articulations of Christian sexual ethics in the twentieth century have come from personalist philosophy. Instead of emphasizing rationally derived rules, personalism focuses on the realities that we perceive through our experience of being human. One of the first personalists was Dietrich von Hildebrand, who fled Germany after opposing Hitler and spent the rest of his years writing and teaching in New York. Von Hildebrand's work – especially his writing on love and the spiritual life – had a great impact on subsequent authors, including Dorothy Day, Pope John Paul II, and Pope Benedict XVI.

In the 1920s, von Hildebrand published *In Defense of Purity,* which has recently been re-released. The book is a meditation on the depth and mystery of sex. In contrast to his contemporaries, who emphasized the dangers of impurity and sin, von Hildebrand's account is grounded in the beauties of purity and virtue.

It begins by preemptively countering one thesis of the sexual revolution: unlike hunger and thirst, sex is "*essentially* deep" and "involves the soul deeply in its passion" (all italics are original). This is because sex is our most intimate act of self-disclosure, "the secret of the individual, which he instinctively hides from others." Therefore, "to disclose and

Nathaniel Peters is the executive director of the Morningside Institute.

Image from Bridgeman Images, New York copyright © 2018 / Artists Rights Society (ARS), New York

surrender it is in a unique sense to surrender oneself." We often talk about finding ourselves. For von Hildebrand, we find ourselves only by giving ourselves away. Only by losing our lives for the sake of love of God and neighbor will we find them. We can find ourselves through sex, therefore, not by the strength of our passion or pleasure, but by the depth with which we offer ourselves to another, body and soul.

The danger of such a gift lies precisely in this power. Because sex is a real and final self-gift, it requires entering into a lasting external union, "a permanent objective community of life." Without such a union, there is a lack of harmony between the objective character of the act – what one is doing – and the intention with which it is performed – why and how one does it. In order to be true to the reality it expresses, sex must take place within the bond and love of marriage.

When it comes to our sexuality, von Hildebrand concludes, we are faced with a mystery on either side: "Either the mysterious union of two human beings takes place in the sight of God . . . or man flings himself away, surrenders his secret, delivers himself over to the flesh, desecrates and violates the secret of another, severs himself in a mysterious fashion from God."

For Christians, marriage is ultimately an expression of the bond between Christ and the Church, as Paul teaches in Ephesians 5. Surrender to a spouse must be formed by surrender to God. Marriage is also a sign of the union between the persons of the Trinity, a union that overflows into the new life of creation. As such, von Hildebrand argues, procreation is a vital part of marriage: "The

> Together, purity and reverence cultivate tenderness.

marriage act can only be transformed qualitatively and ennobled from within when the immensely powerful thought of the inception of a new human soul influences the physical act of sex through the medium of wedded love." This is not to say that infertile couples do not have real marriages. Rather, Christians should cultivate an openness to receiving children as gifts from God. They are not an optional accessory to marriage, like a dog or a cat.

Having laid out his understanding of human sexuality, von Hildebrand turns to the definition of purity. Contemporary Christians tend to think of purity as a matter of guarding one's heart and body so as to give them to a future spouse unstained. For von Hildebrand, however, purity is a matter of union with and conformity to Christ. "It is the surrender to this splendor [of God] which formally *constitutes* purity," he writes. The soul of a pure person is marked by radiance and clarity, full of love and humble sincerity, living in the world illuminated by the light of God's truth.

"Reverence is a fundamental component of purity," von Hildebrand continues. Purity is not prudery or insensibility. Rather, the pure person clearly sees the powerful mysteries of God and loves them rightly. To borrow a metaphor from art history, the pure person's solution to the danger of lust is not to put fig leaves on statues, but to look at nudes that faithfully depict the beauty of the human form.

Together, purity and reverence cultivate tenderness. Of all the traits von Hildebrand discusses, tenderness is most conspicuous in its absence from the fruits of the sexual revolution, as the *New Yorker* story "Cat Person" and contemporary TV shows and films attest. Tenderness requires truly willing the good of the other, reverence for the other, and vulnerability – the kind of things that casual sex destroys. Hence, von Hildebrand writes, "It is now clear what sex is as exercised by the pure: an unconstrained, tenderly affectionate surrender of love grounded in a humble, reverent, serene, and radiant attitude. No sultry heats are here, nor grossness of triumphant flesh."

This is true, in a sense, but also shows the drawbacks of *In Defense of Purity*. Von Hildebrand's writing can seem maudlin to a modern reader – the prose equivalent of a German drawing room from the 1920s. In exalting the spiritual nature of marital love, he sometimes misses its earthiness and humanity. Sex may elevate raw physical desires, but it does not escape them. It is hard to see how von Hildebrand accounts for the comedy of marital love, the fact that one can burst out laughing in the middle of it. Yet that humor, physicality, and humanity are precisely what make Christian marriage participate in the mystery of the Incarnation, when Christ took on our human nature in all its curious aspects.

Furthermore, in the century since *In Defense of Purity* was written, other philosophers have given accounts of Christian sexual ethics, chief among them John Paul II's *Love and Responsibility* and "Theology of the Body." Contemporary authors such as J. Budziszewski and Alexander Pruss offer arguments for the intrinsic meaning of sex that go beyond von Hildebrand, largely because today we require those arguments in a way his audience did not.

Finally, von Hildebrand turns to the question of consecrated virginity. He argues that the person who does not find a spouse is not necessarily purer than the one who does. What the church values is not celibacy, per se, but consecrated virginity, which is freely chosen and sealed with vows like a marriage. Consecrated virginity is a spiritual marriage with Christ. The church considers it the highest vocation, not because sex is dirty, but "because as a state of life it is the *expression* freely chosen as such of what is essentially the final and supreme vocation of every man."

> Tenderness requires truly willing the good of the other, reverence for the other, and vulnerability.

I reflected on this when a friend of mine made her final profession as a Dominican nun this fall. My own marriage reflects the reality of Christ's espousal of the church, but Sister Diana Marie's consecrated life reflects the reality that our souls ultimately belong to Christ alone, now and forever.

When I was in Buffalo for her final profession, I told the hotel's shuttle driver the reason for my visit. He couldn't fathom the life she had chosen: "Having just one woman for the rest of your life – that's a good thing, right?" Yes, I replied, and held up my wedding ring, I'm doing that myself. But Sister Diana Marie has chosen a different kind of marriage. (No watching football games either, he was stunned to hear, though I assured him that nuns relax in other ways.) "So it would be kind of like going to church on Sunday, and giving God part of your time, but then staying in church with the same people, all the time?" Yes, a bit like that. It is a total consecration to God, all the time, a heightened way to live the baptism all Christians have and a foretaste of what we hope to enjoy forever. For the vision of God is the end goal of all Christian lives, and the greatest fruit of purity. ➤

READING

Definition of a Good Farmer

PHILIP BRITTS

Asuka Hishiki, *Turnips*

A good farmer is one who:

1. Realizes that his farm is an organic unit in which all the organs must function in cooperation and reciprocation.

2. Realizes that the fertility of the soil is the life-blood of his farm and that this fertility is not static, but is a dynamic and perishable balance.

3. Realizes that humus is the mainspring of fertility.

4. Realizes that for each part of the farm there is a best natural use of the land, and conforms to it as far as possible.

5. Realizes that climate is the most powerful single factor affecting crop production; that it cannot be controlled, and should not be fought against, but cooperated with.

6. Fights insects and diseases firstly by prevention and uses poison sprays, dusts, etc., with caution and reluctance.

7. Realizes that grass is the earth's most important crop, takes care of his permanent pastures, and uses temporary pastures to protect and replenish his soil.

8. Realizes the importance of the genetic constitution of his plants and animals, and makes use of breeding to improve quality.

9. Has the energy, tenacity, and organizing ability to keep the farm clean and tidy, and to keep clear records.

10. Realizes that he knows next to nothing of all that there is to know, that he is dealing with eternal laws that he did not make and cannot alter, and that the most brilliant achievements of human knowledge are simply the closest obedience to these laws. ⤳

Philip Britts (1917–1949) was a horticulturalist and poet. The article above is excerpted from a new book featuring his essays and poetry, Water at the Roots: Poems and Insights of a Visionary Farmer *(Plough, March 2018).* plough.com/britts

Photograph by Saul Cuellar / Unsplash

Sightings

DWIGHT WAREHAM

I WAS CLEARING VEGETATION from around tree seedlings and shrubs that I was trying to encourage in the nature preserve, a five-acre area that the first- and second-graders I teach at the Bruderhof school have been developing as a wildlife habitat. While working, I was surprised to notice an eastern cottontail sitting motionless in a little hideout underneath some dried-up ferns about five feet from where I stood. I stopped working and stalked quite a bit closer before it hopped away to safety. The next day I forgot all about it until I was working in the same area and again found it in exactly the same location. In the days and months following, it was frequently seen resting in its matted-down hideout. One day, with my whole class watching, I crawled slowly toward the eastern cottontail to pet it and got my hand within eight inches of its

back before it again hopped to a safer place. Later, my son managed to get four inches away. It would not be touched. After that we left it alone.

Yesterday I saw a fawn lying on one of the islands of Low Pond. It was in the shade of a twelve-foot white pine and only its head and ears were visible above the thick vegetation.

Today I saw a doe with her fawn walking through the witch hazel woods northeast of Low Pond in our nature preserve. As I followed them, I heard an interesting chattering noise that sounded something like a yellow-billed cuckoo. I went to investigate and discovered a baby raccoon about ten inches long, not counting the tail. I watched it search for shelter from a rain shower under a skunk cabbage leaf and a fallen log on the stream bank.

Dwight Wareham is an avid naturalist and a veteran elementary school teacher. He lives at the Mount Community, a Bruderhof in Esopus, NY.

Gerrard Winstanley and the Diggers

JASON LANDSEL

King Charles I was beheaded in January 1649, as England reeled from seven years of civil war: "One third part of England lies waste and barren, and her children starve for want," wrote Gerrard Winstanley (1609–1676).

But Winstanley, a failed cloth merchant turned utopian visionary, had a proposal: "If the lands of England were cooperatively manured by her children it could become, in a few years, the richest, the strongest, and the most flourishing land in the world." Acting on this vision, Winstanley led the "Diggers," a group of men frustrated by taxation, eviction, and hunger, to reclaim common lands on St. George's Hill, in Surrey, where they established a makeshift community.

Before the English Civil War, Winstanley had been comfortably established in London's cloth trade. But the war destroyed the industry, throwing Winstanley into financial ruin and spiritual crisis. He lost faith in the established church: "The subtle clergy know that if they can but charm the people by their divining doctrine to wait for riches, heaven, and glory when they are dead, then they shall easily be the inheritors of the earth, and have the deceived commoners to be their slaves."

What was true faith, then? Winstanley heard the answer while in a trance: "Work together; eat bread together. Declare this all abroad." He began to envision a classless, propertyless society: "The great Creator (whom some call God) made the earth to be a common treasury. Man was to govern this creation. . . . But thanks to covetousness, man was brought into bondage. He became a greater slave to others of his own kind than the beasts of the field were to him. When once the earth becomes a common treasury again, as it must, then strife in all lands will cease."

> "In the beginning of time, all men were equal. It was when self-love arose that man began to fall."
>
> Gerrard Winstanley

But local landlords, threatened by the actions and radical beliefs of these Diggers or "Levelers," attacked the group. Brought to trial for trespass, Winstanley was found guilty and fined. Despite such setbacks, the movement grew. Soon there were at least ten Digger communities throughout the south Midlands. When some became violent, Winstanley distanced himself from them, insisting that "true Levelers" eschewed all violence.

By the end of 1650, however, all the Digger communities had been destroyed, and their followers dispersed. Winstanley went on to join the Quakers, who shared many of his ideals.

His movement may have failed, but Winstanley's vision has inspired many in the four centuries since his death. Today, in a time of growing inequality, his words remain a call to action: "If thou wouldst know what true freedom is, thou shalt see that it lies in the community of spirit and community in the earthly treasury."

Jason Landsel is the artist for Plough's *"Forerunners" series, including the painting opposite.*